COLORING BOOKS FOR ADULTS RELAXATION

Mindfulness

MANDALA, FLOWERS GARDEN AND DOODLE DESIGNS

I0391083

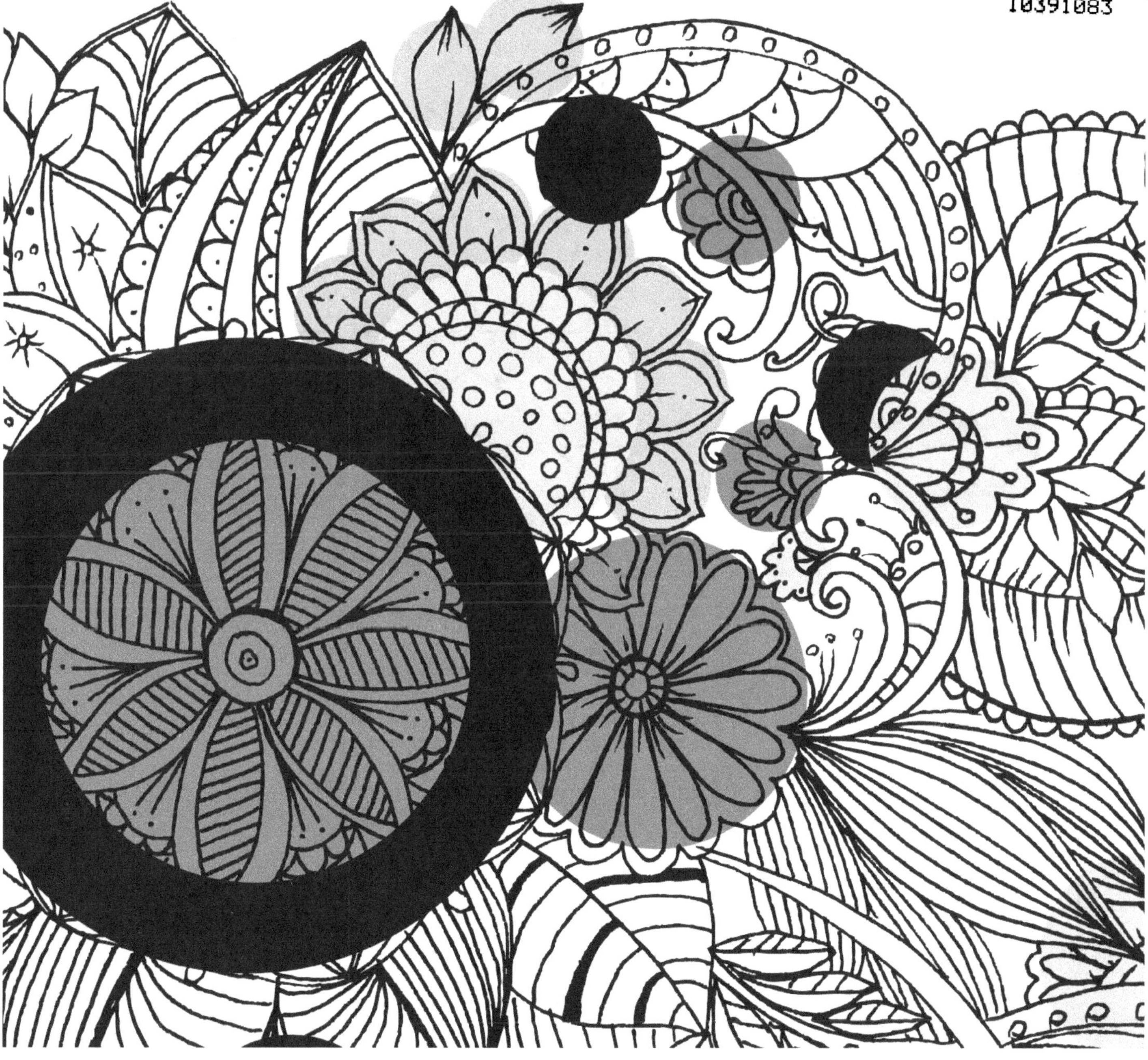

TEST YOUR COLOR

TEST YOUR COLOR

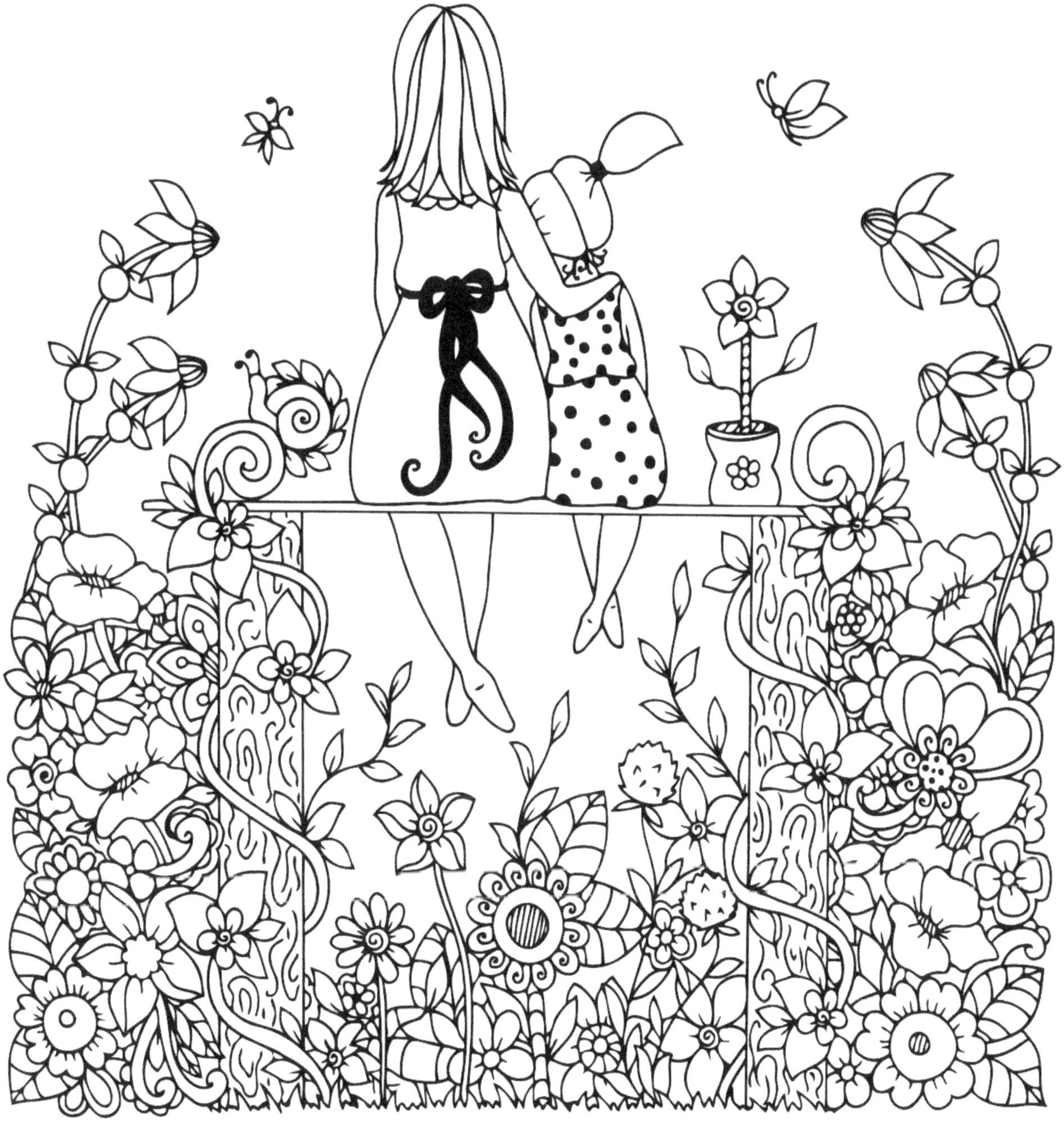

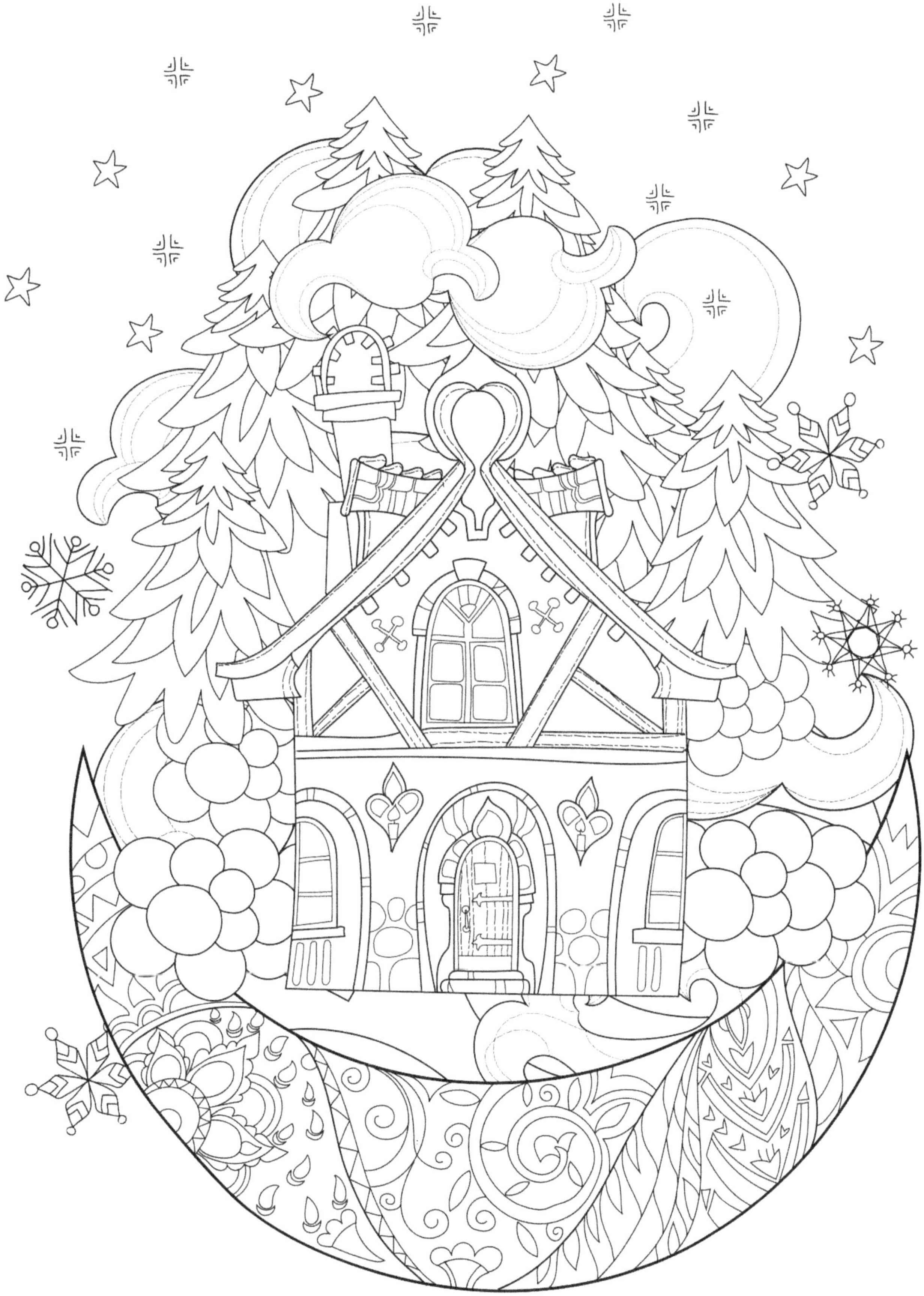

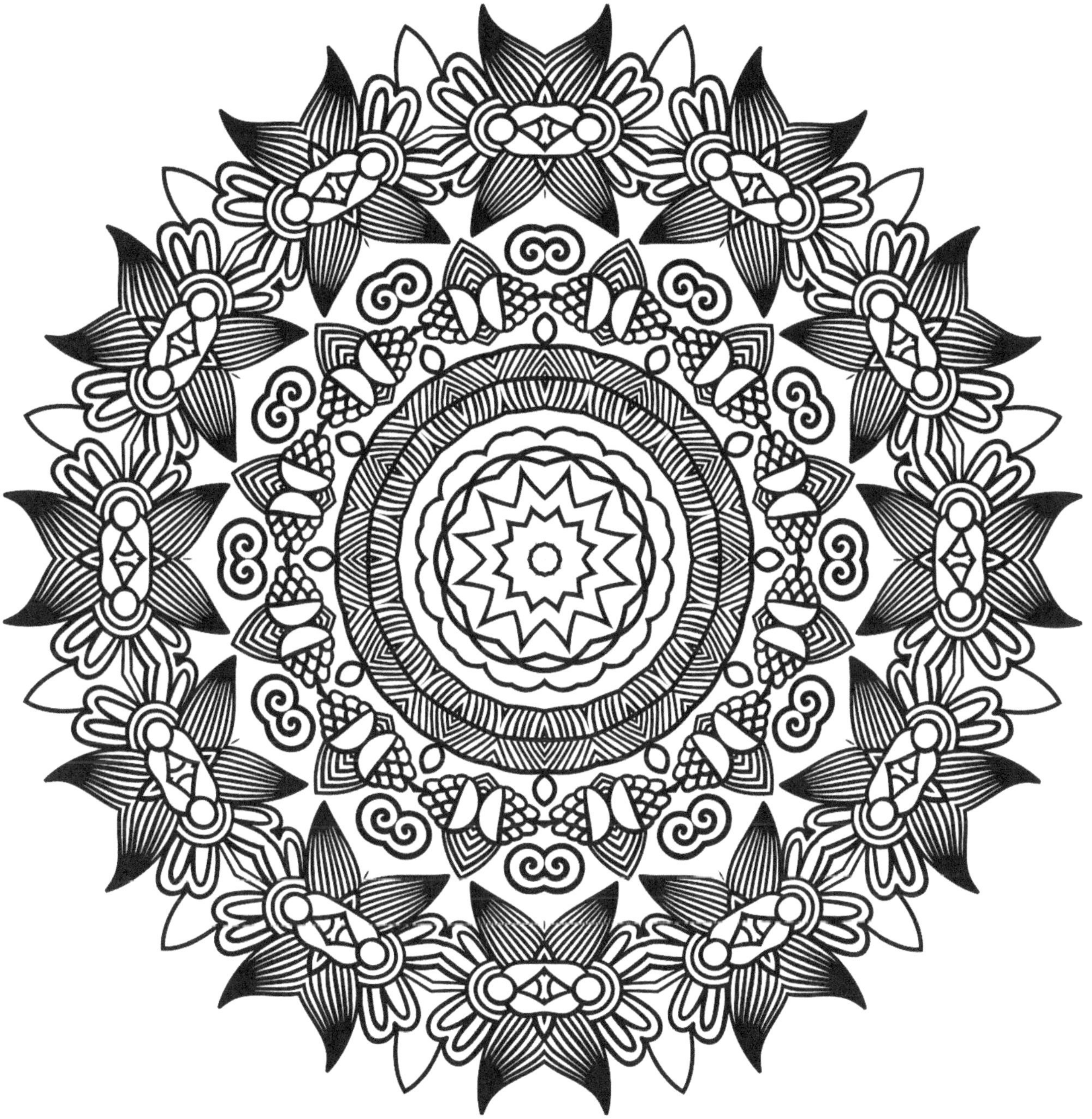

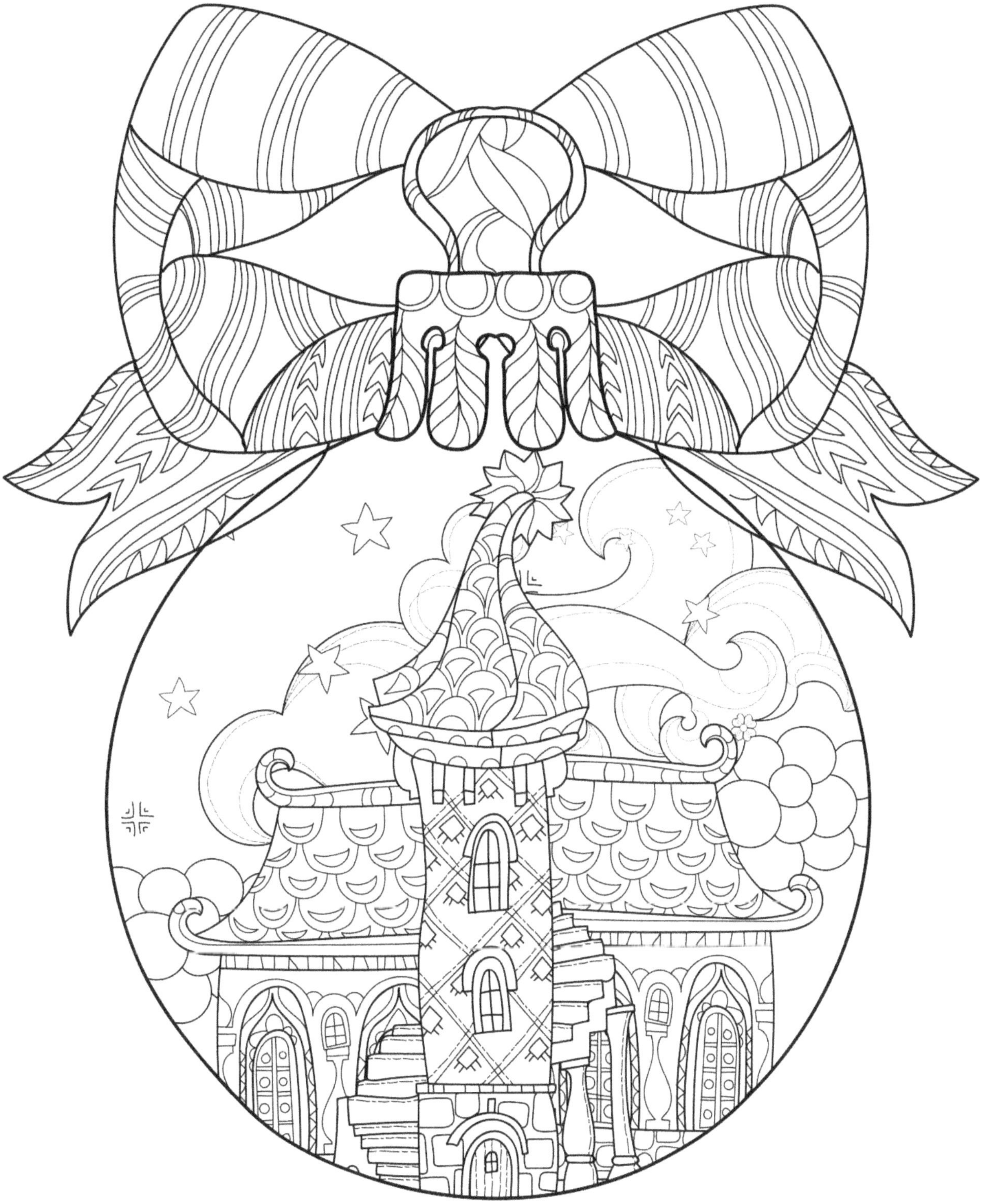

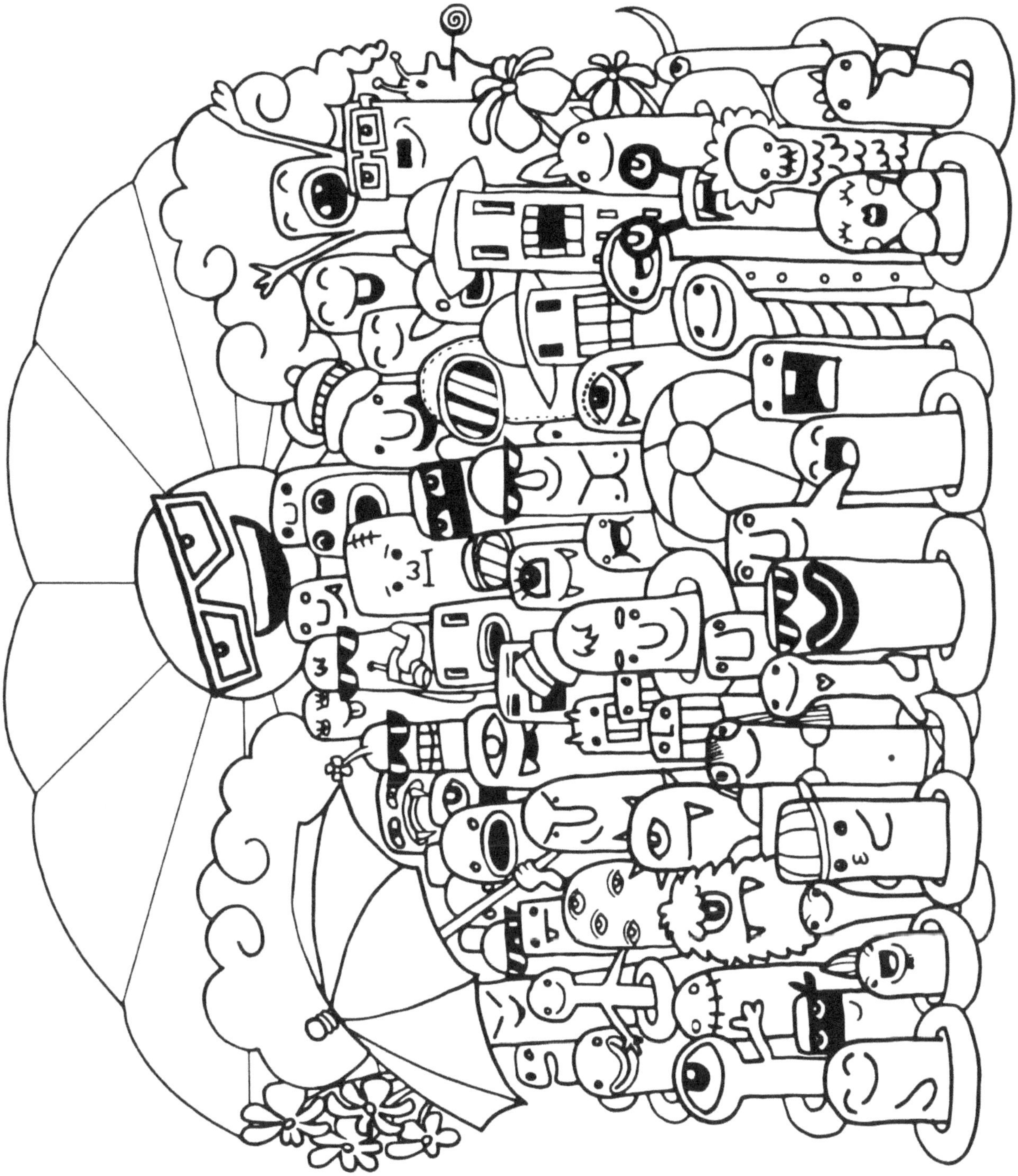

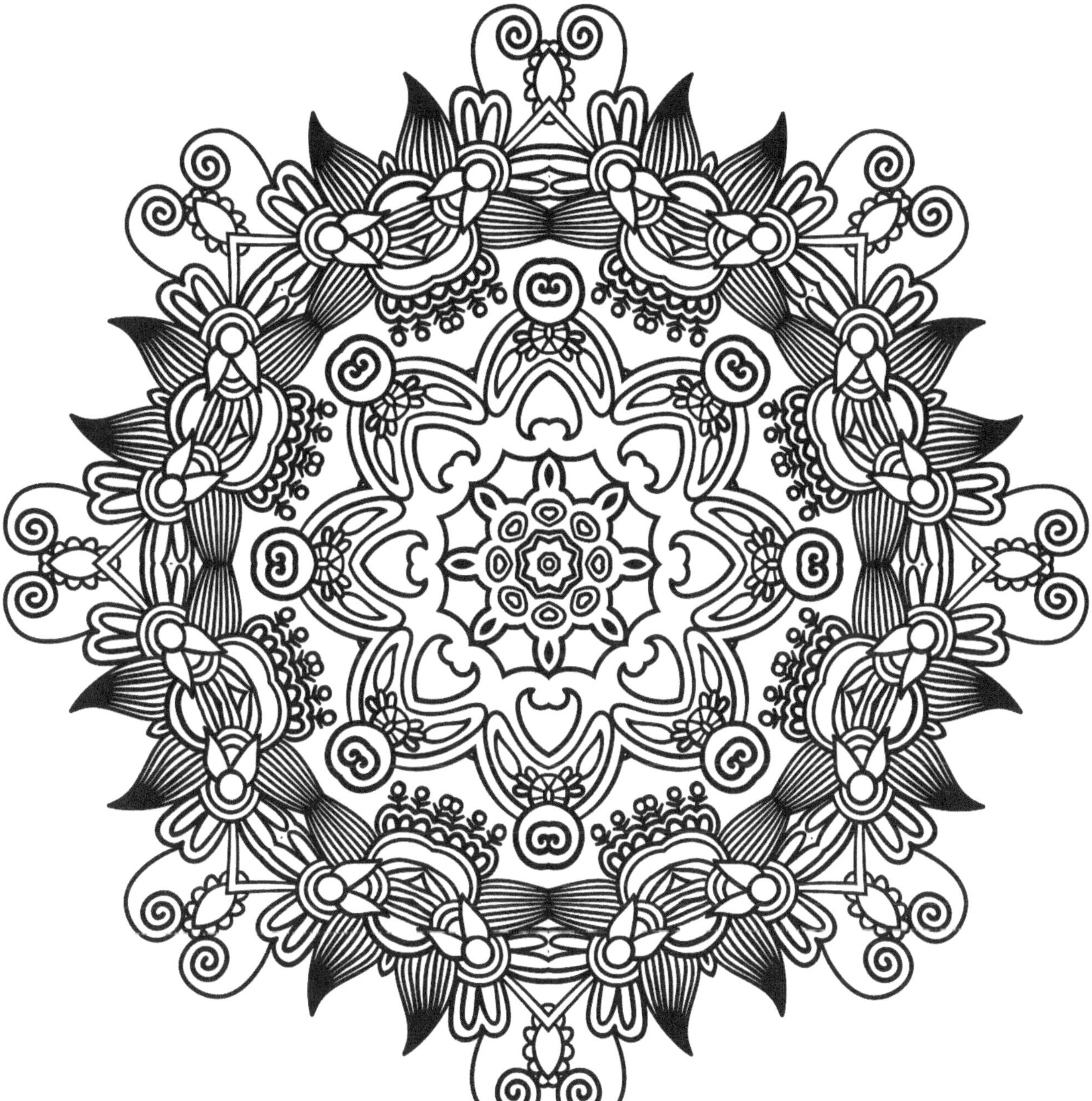

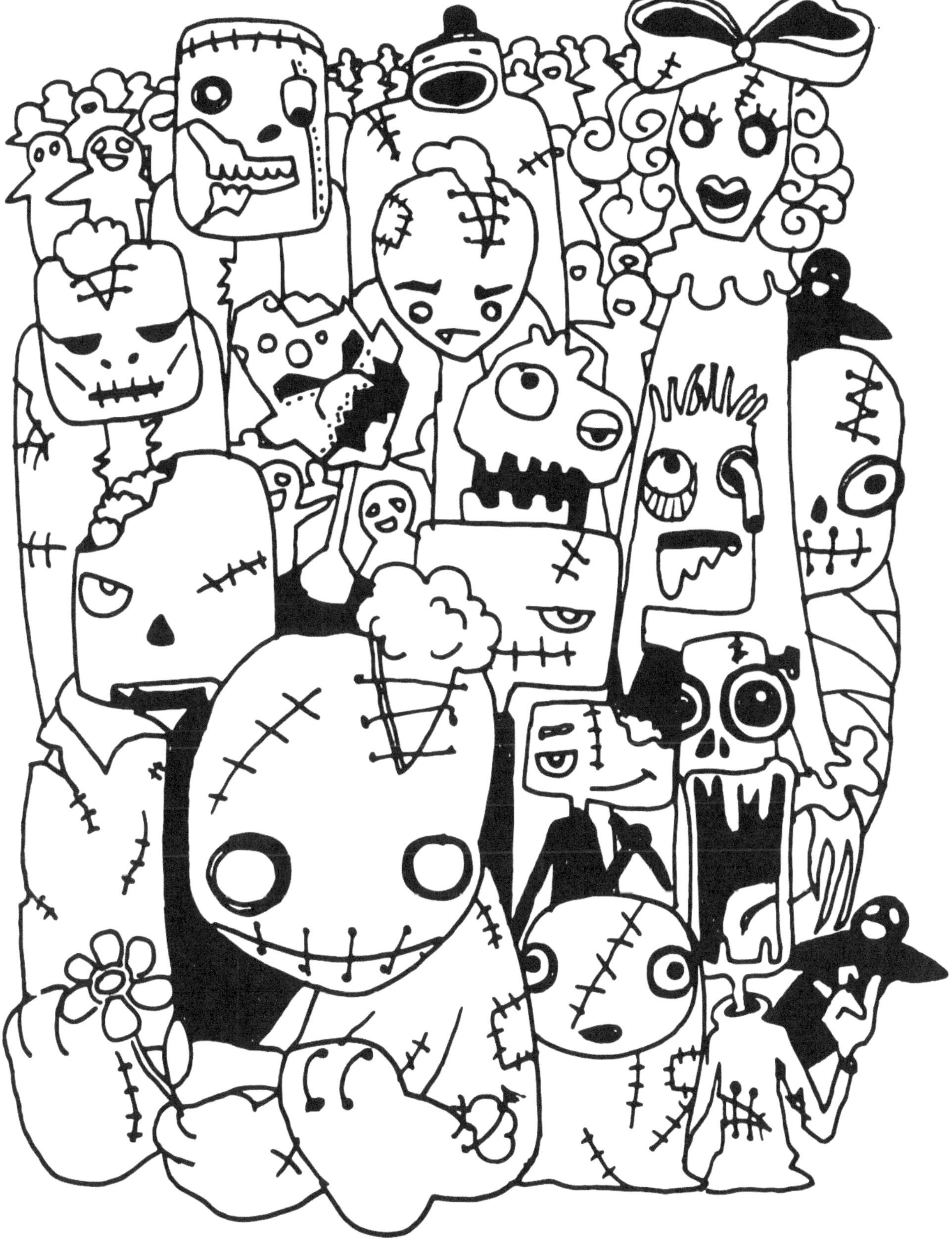

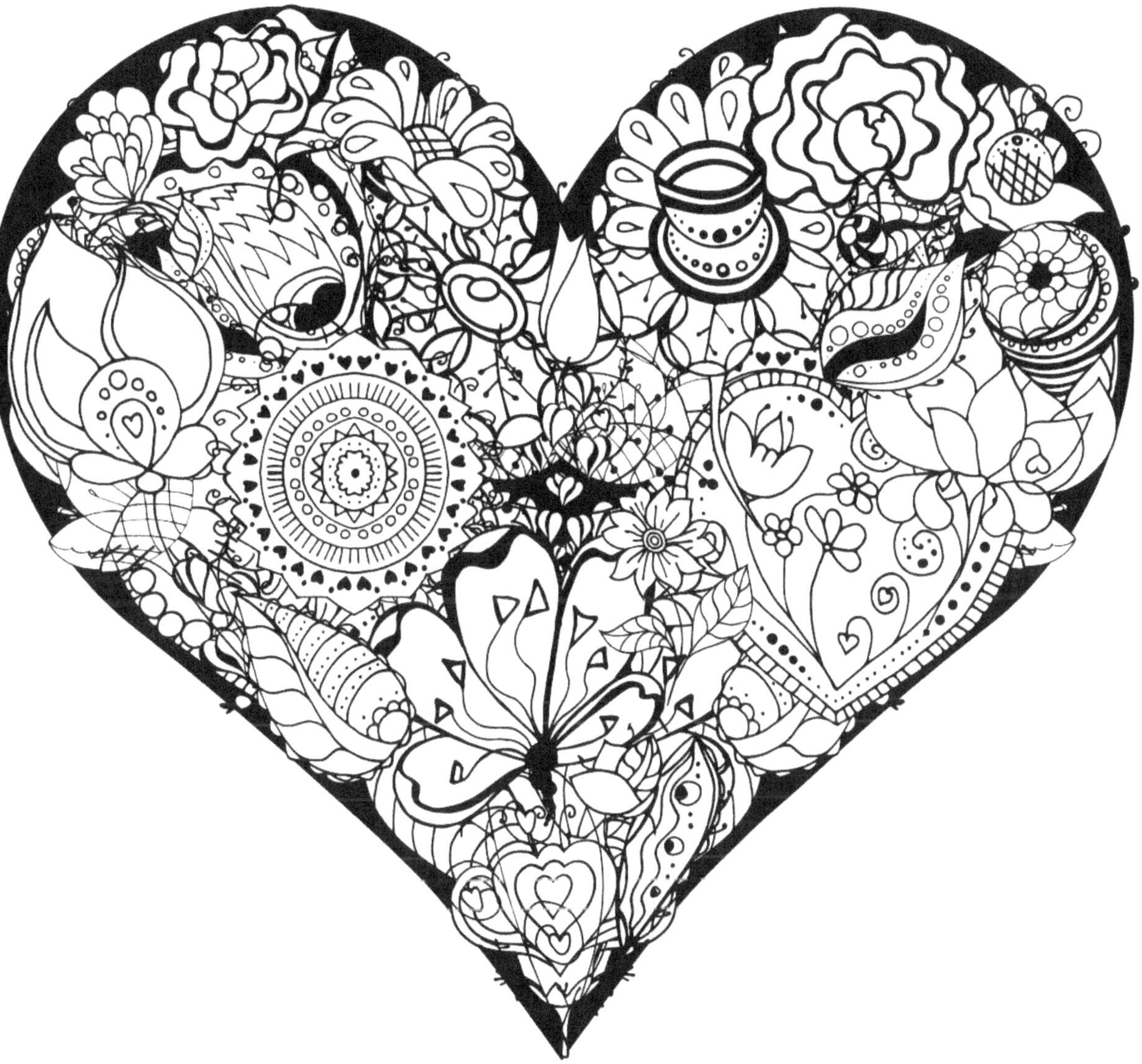

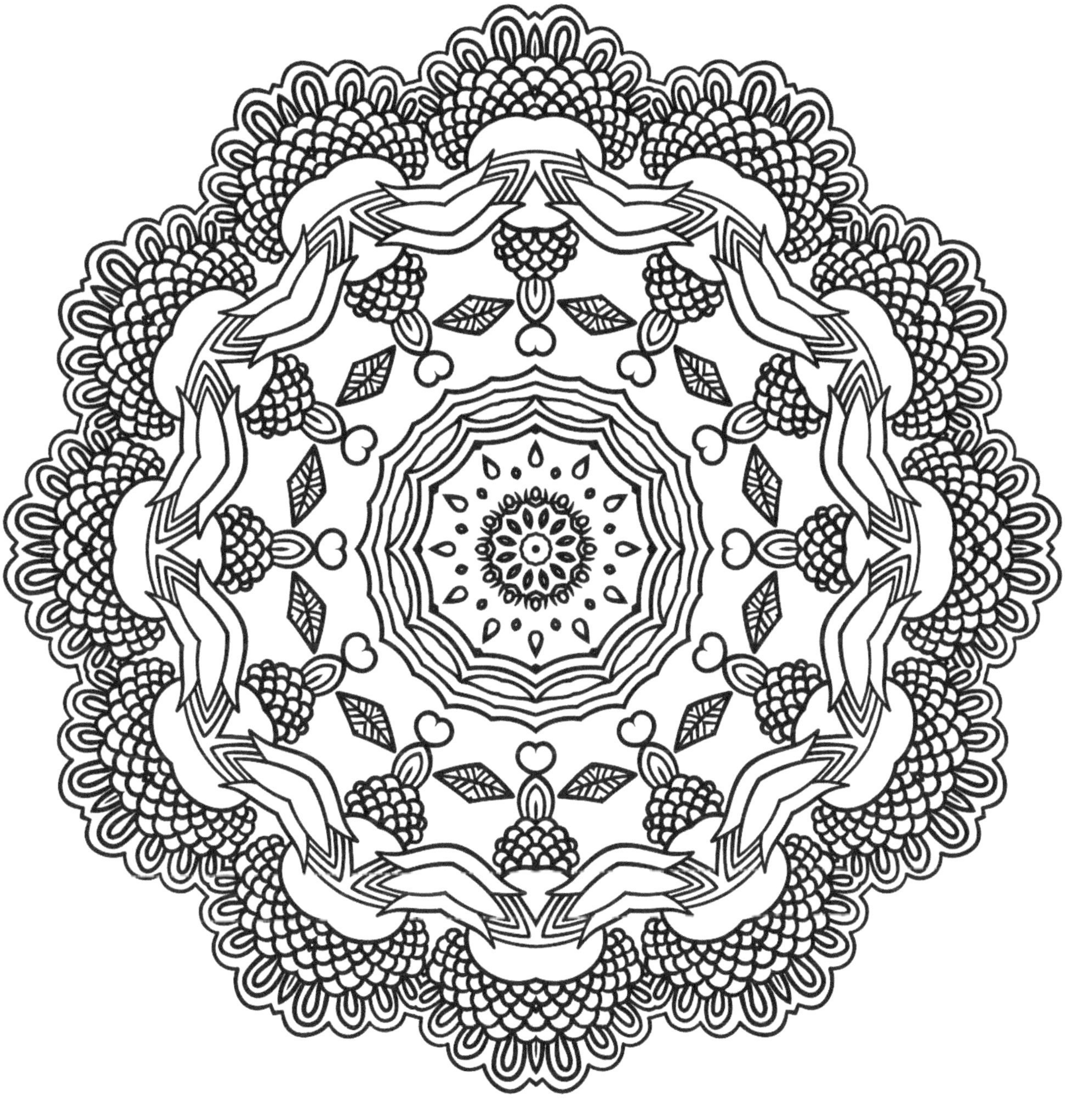

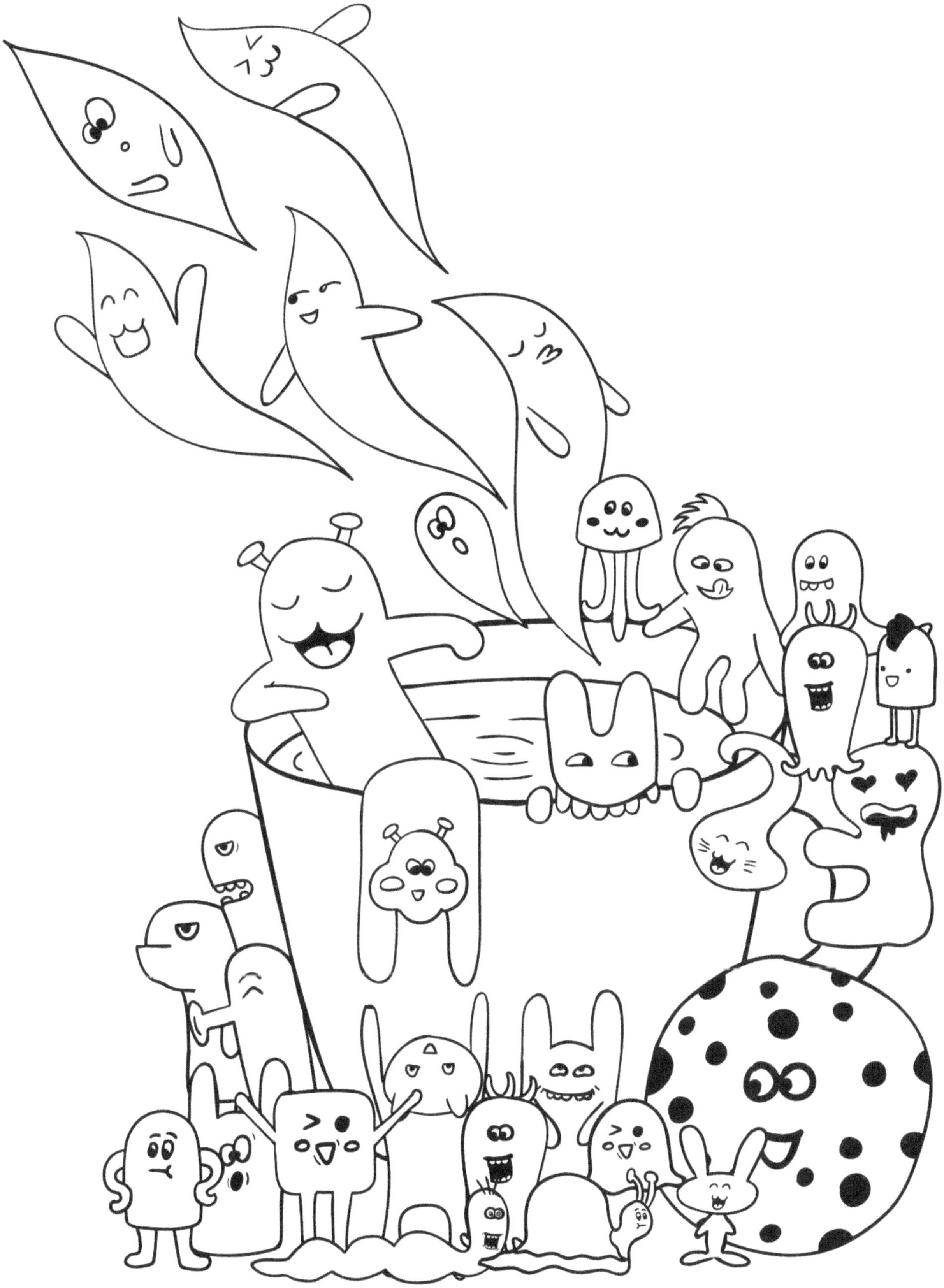

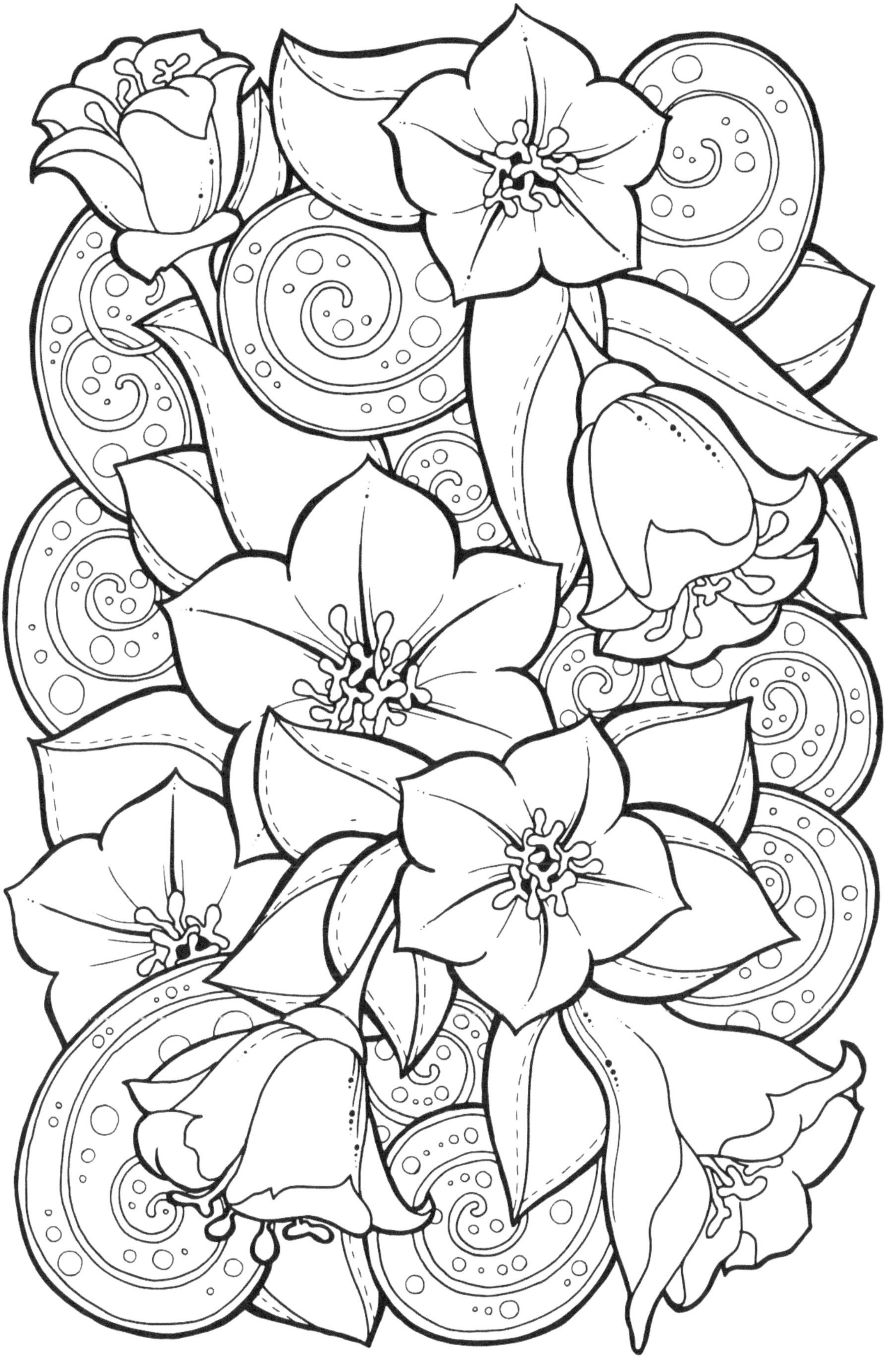

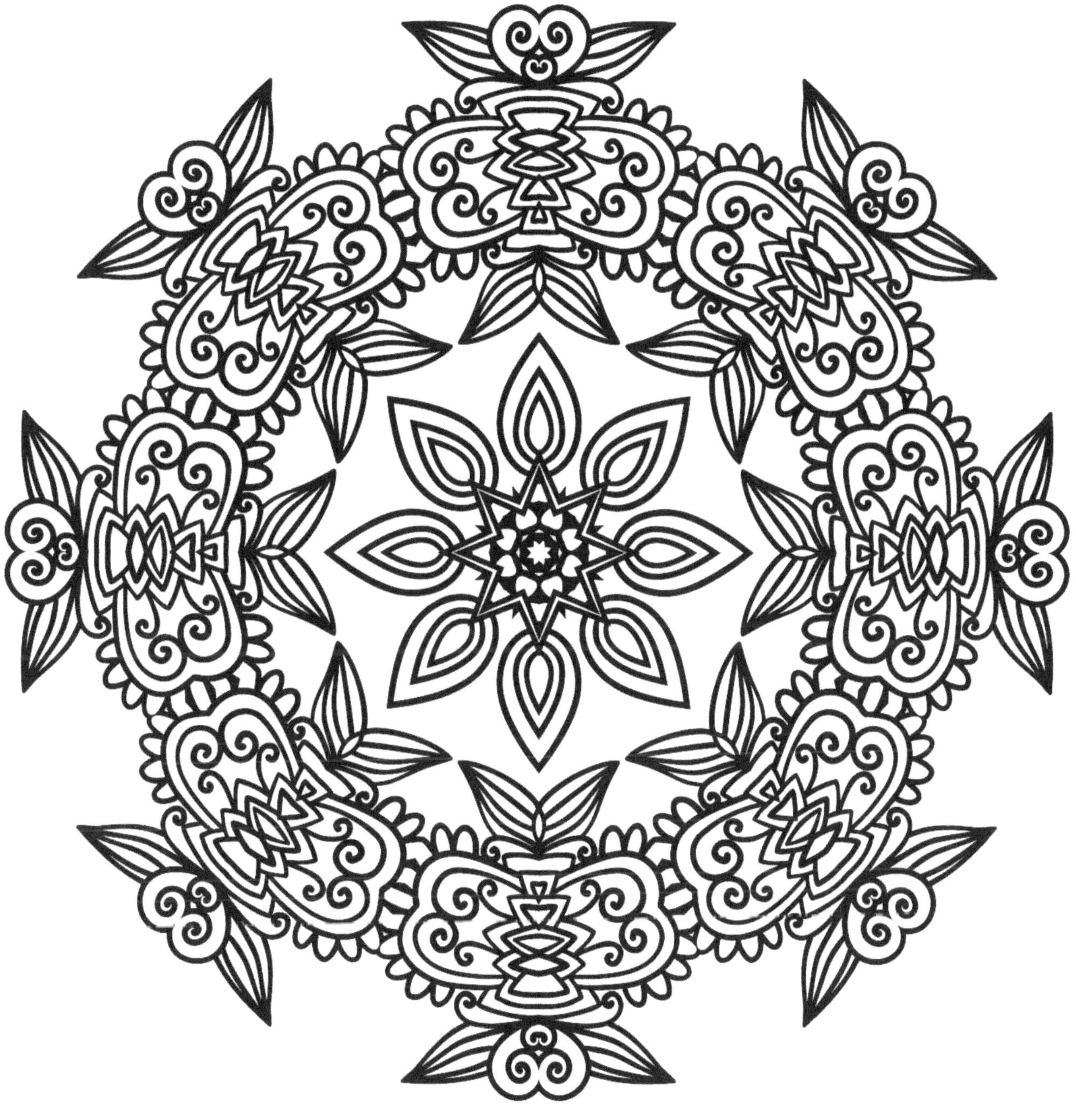

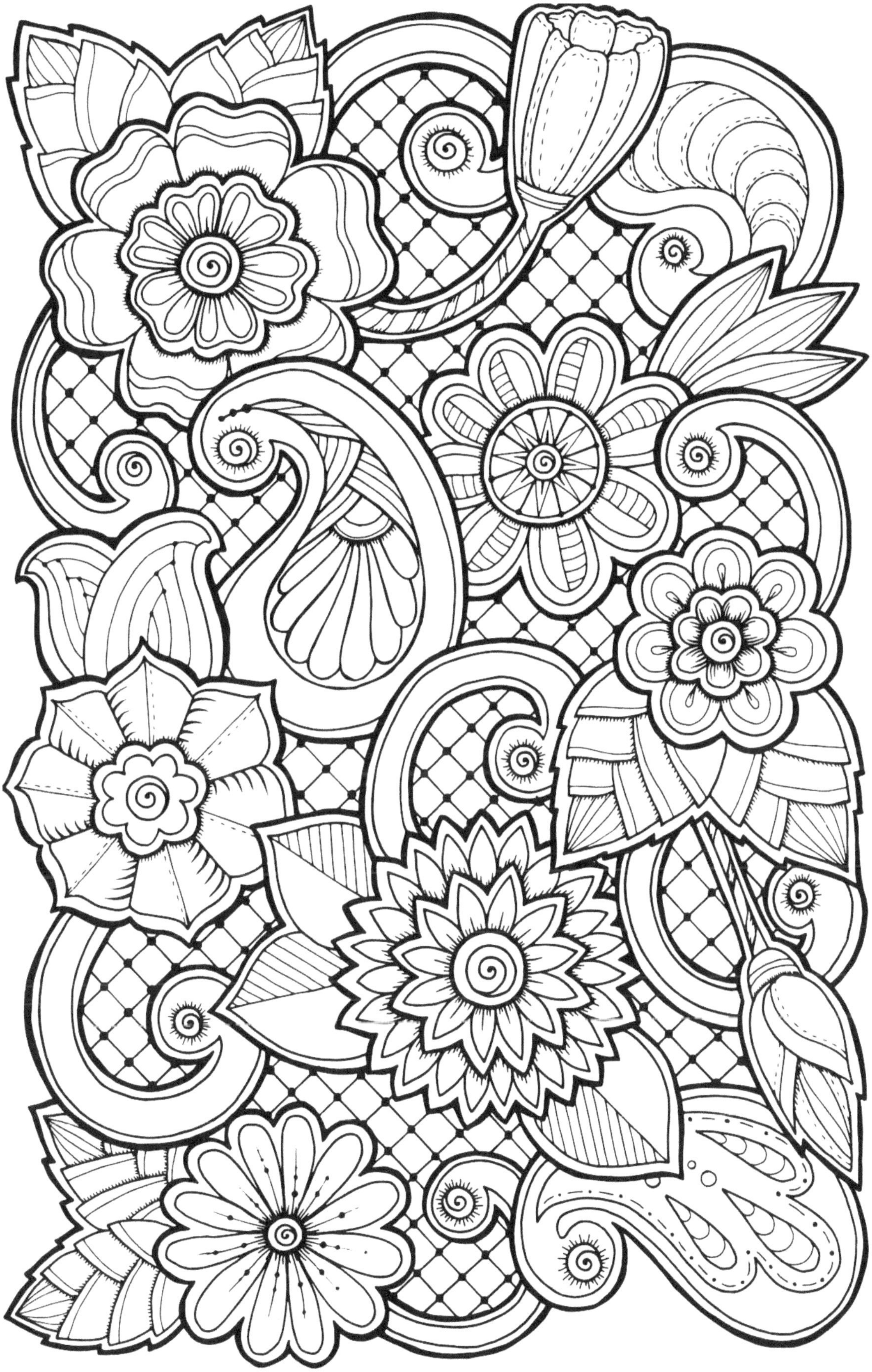

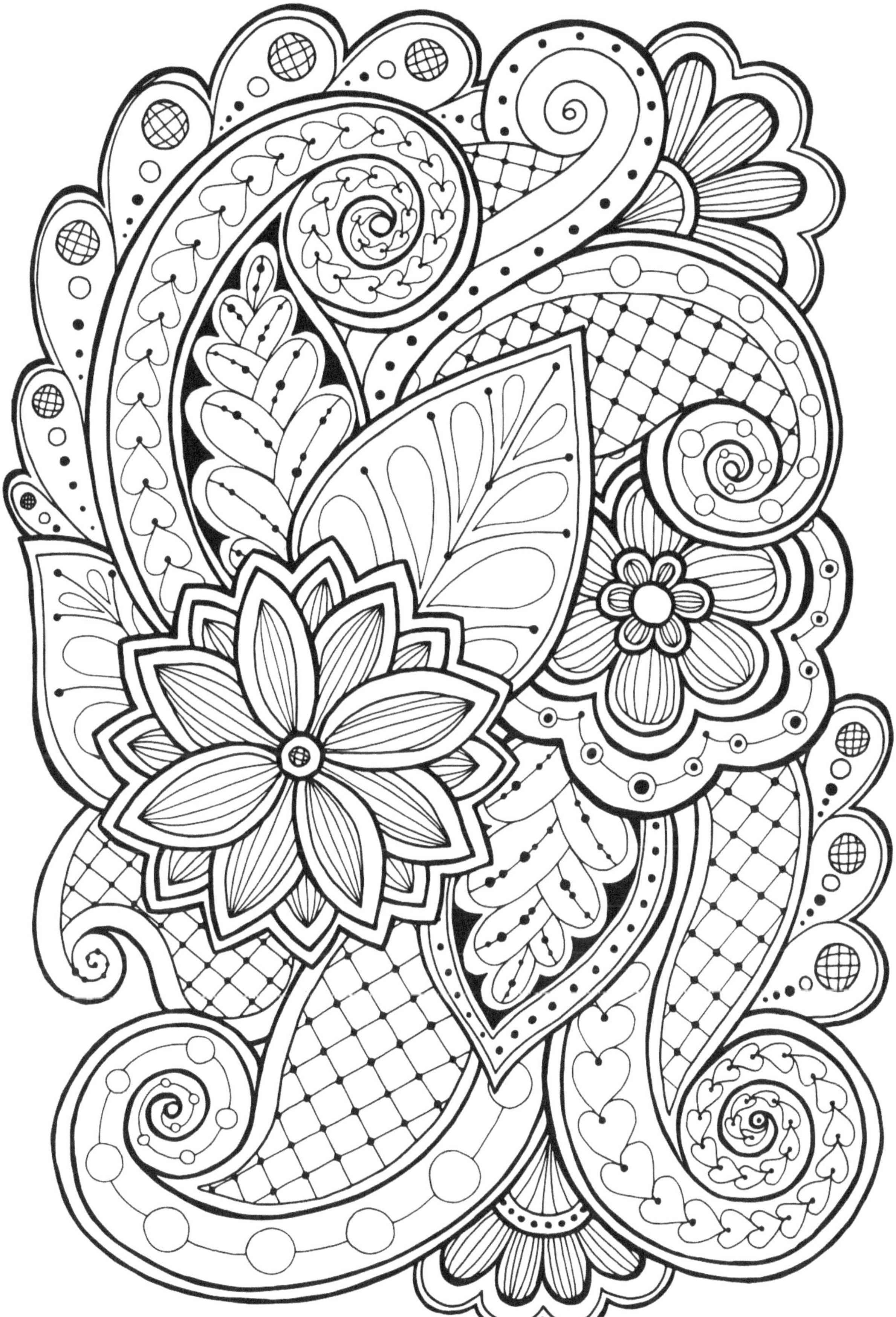

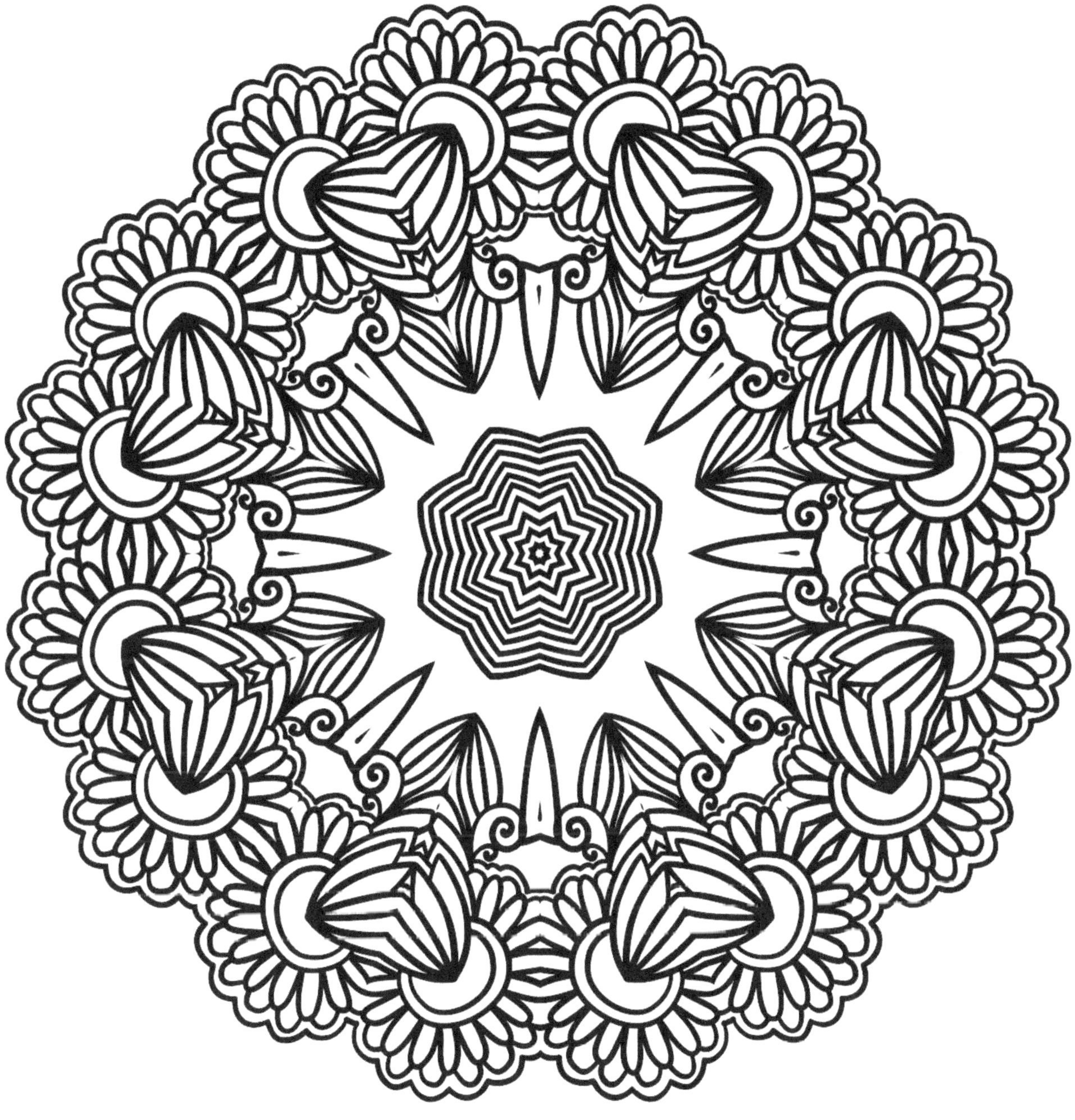

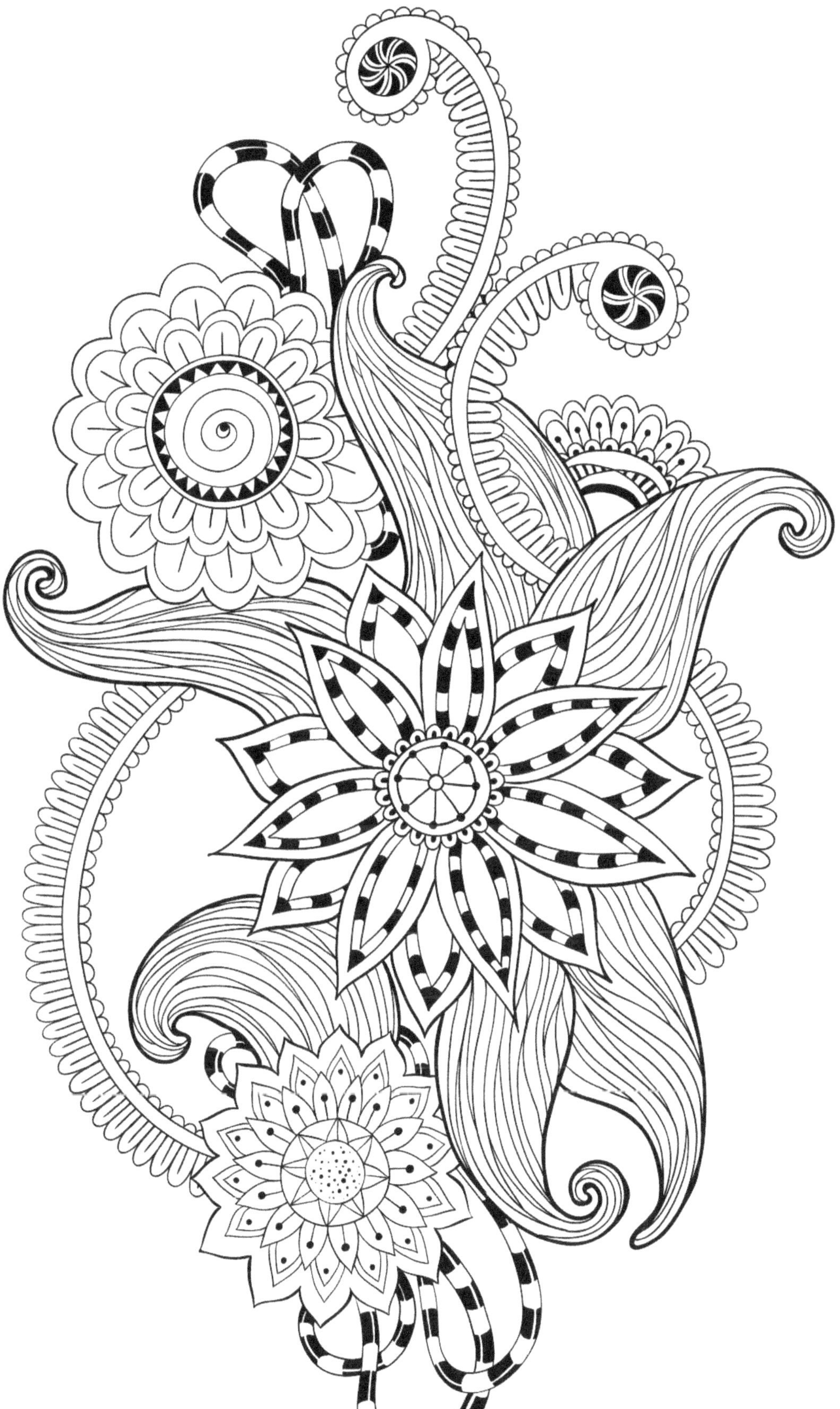

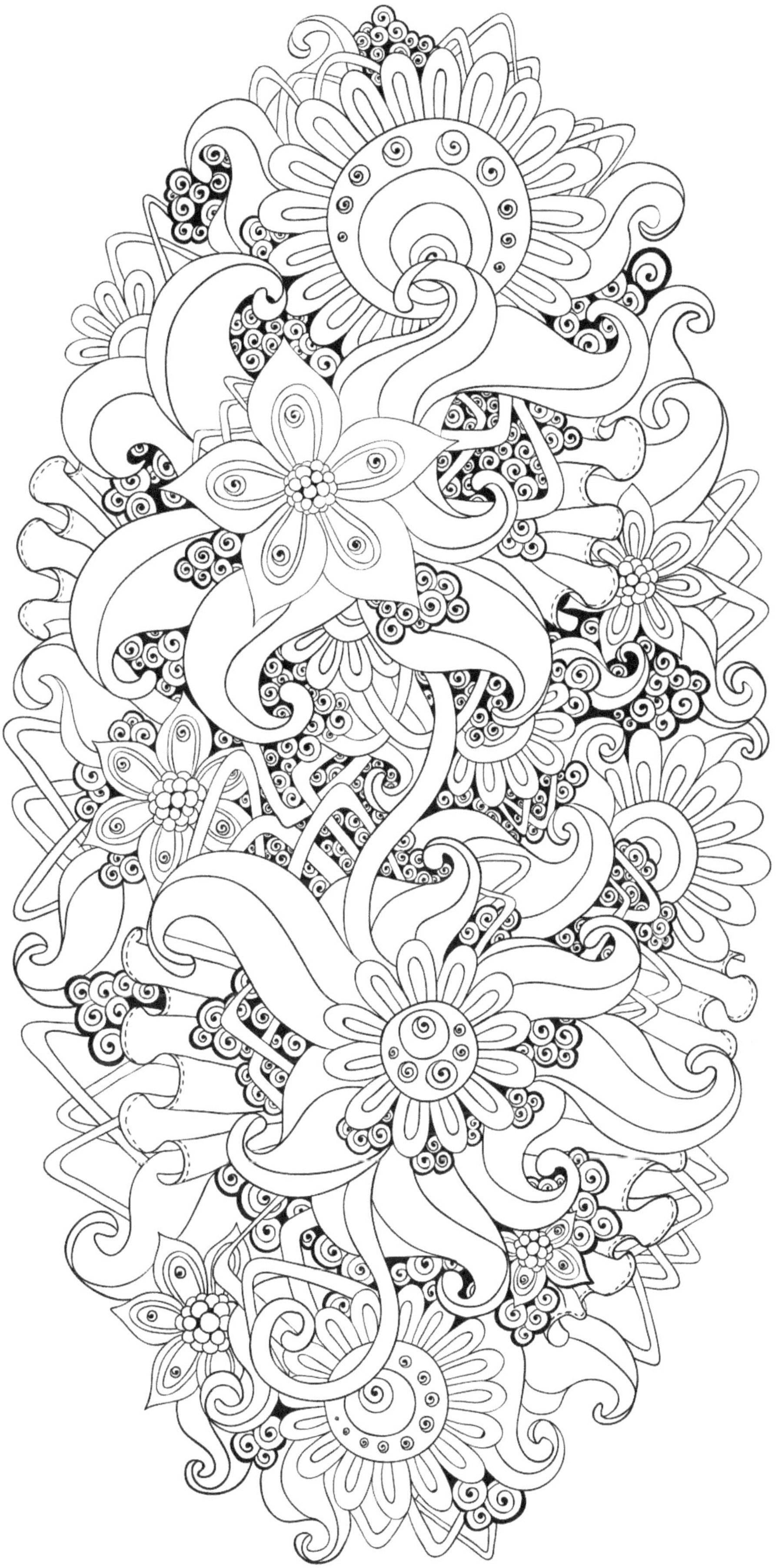

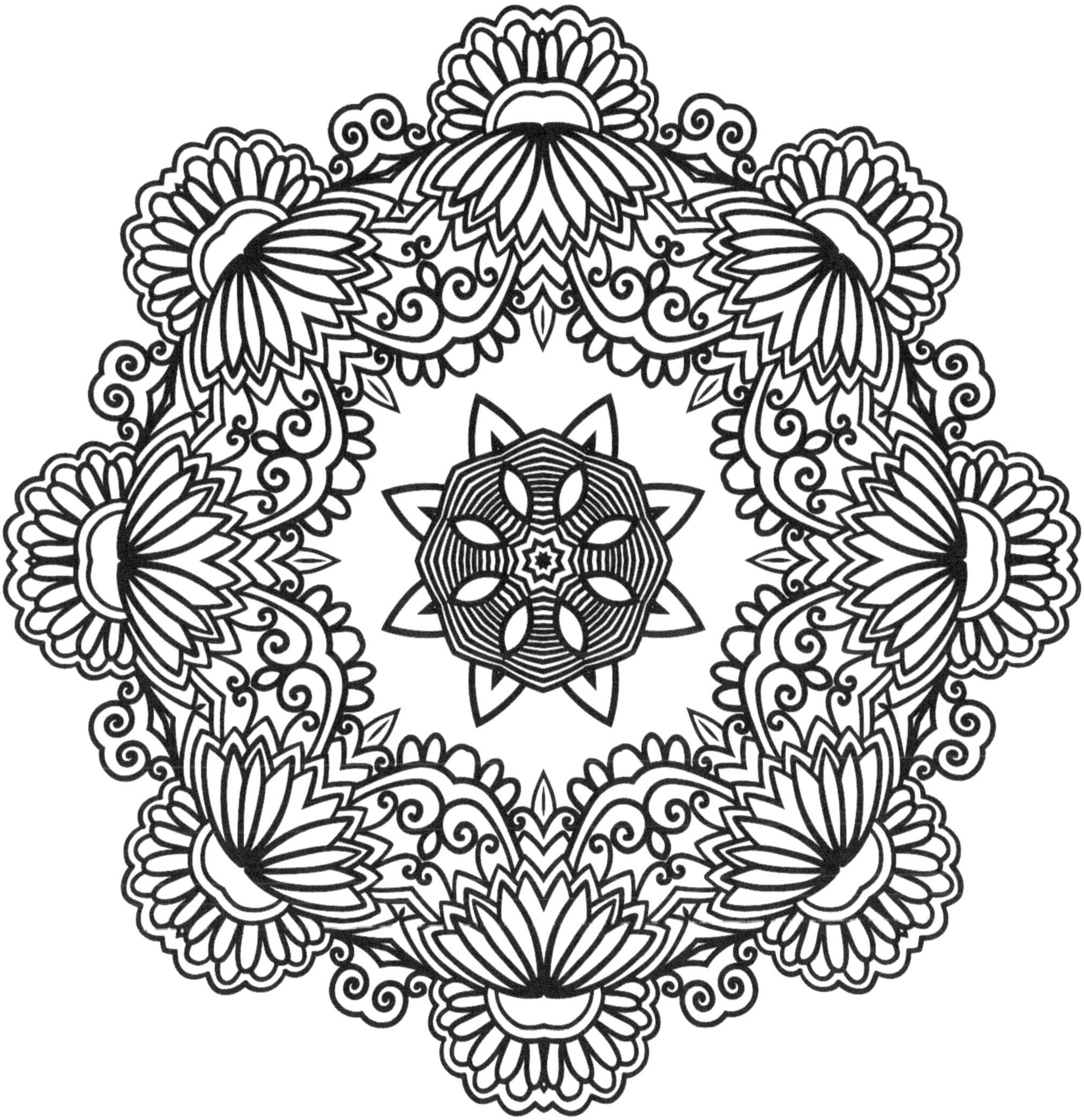

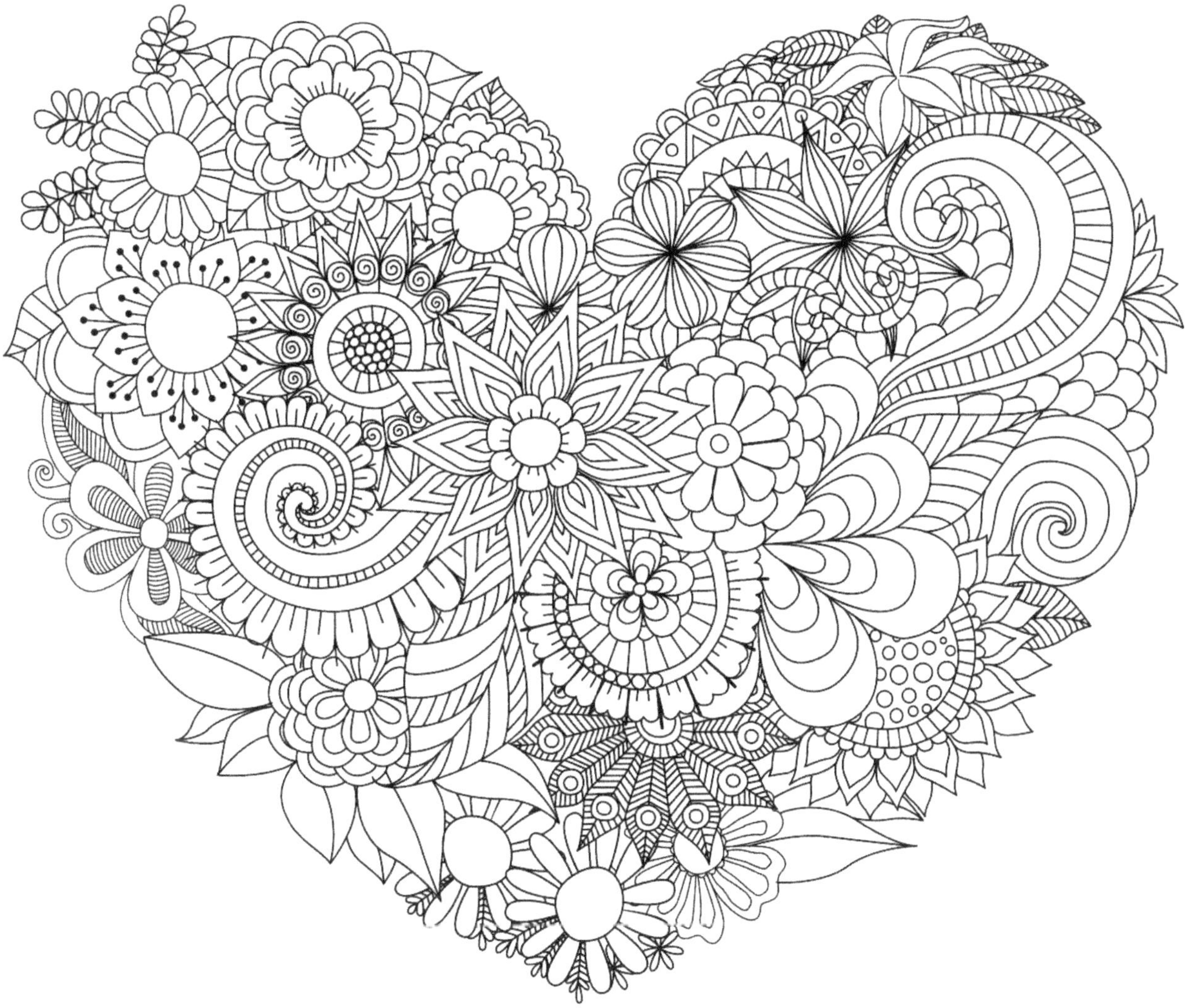

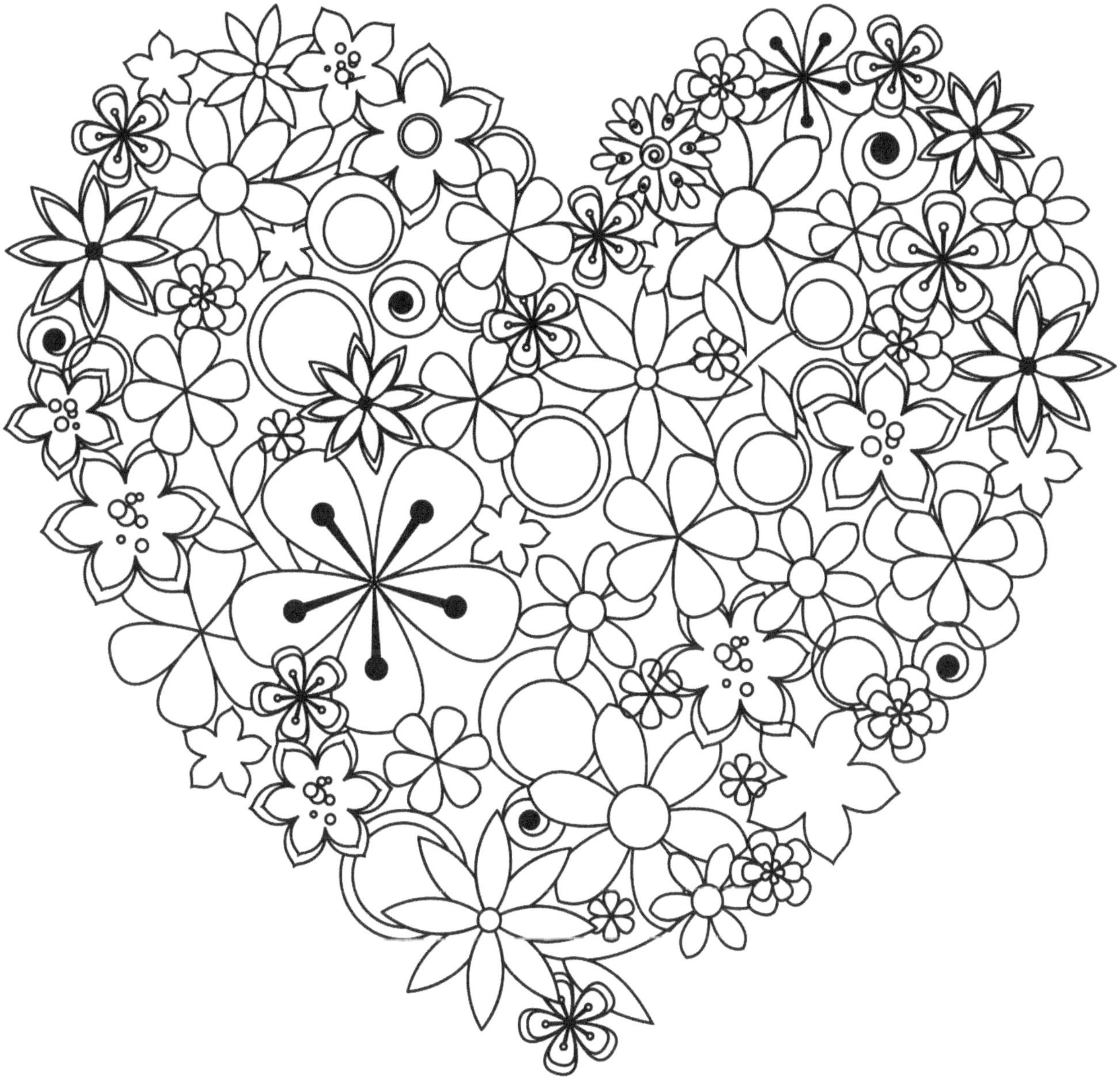

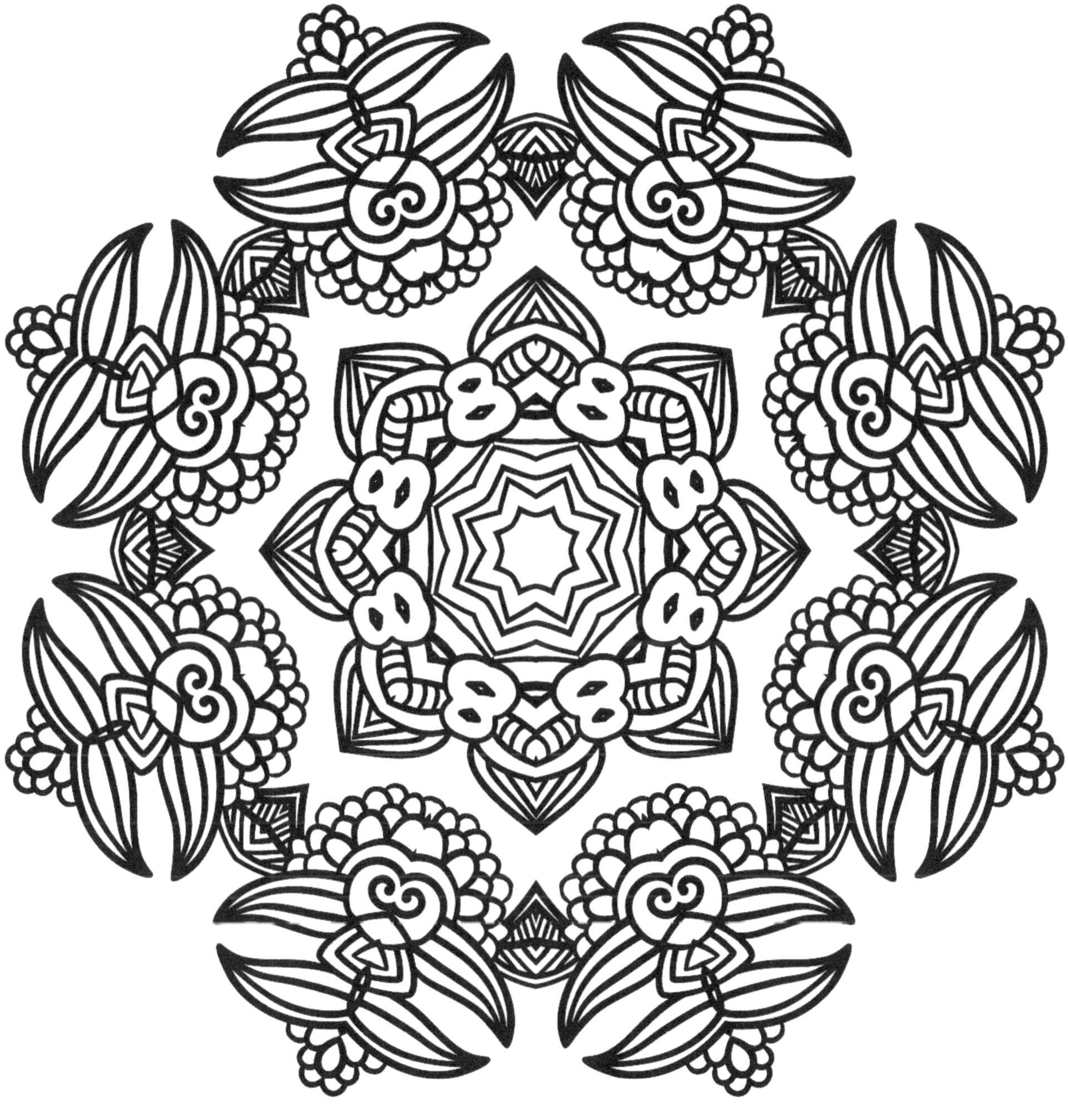

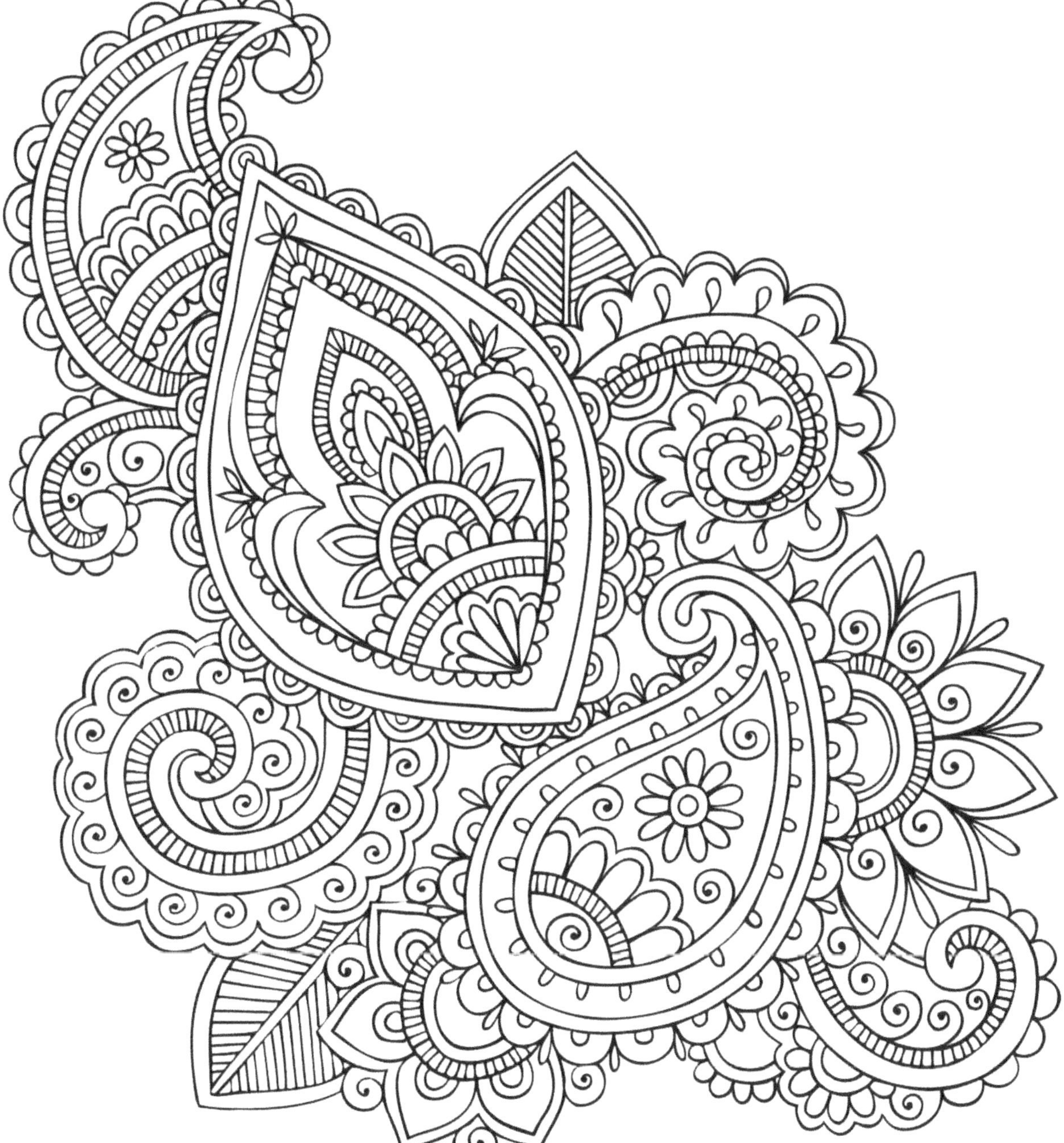

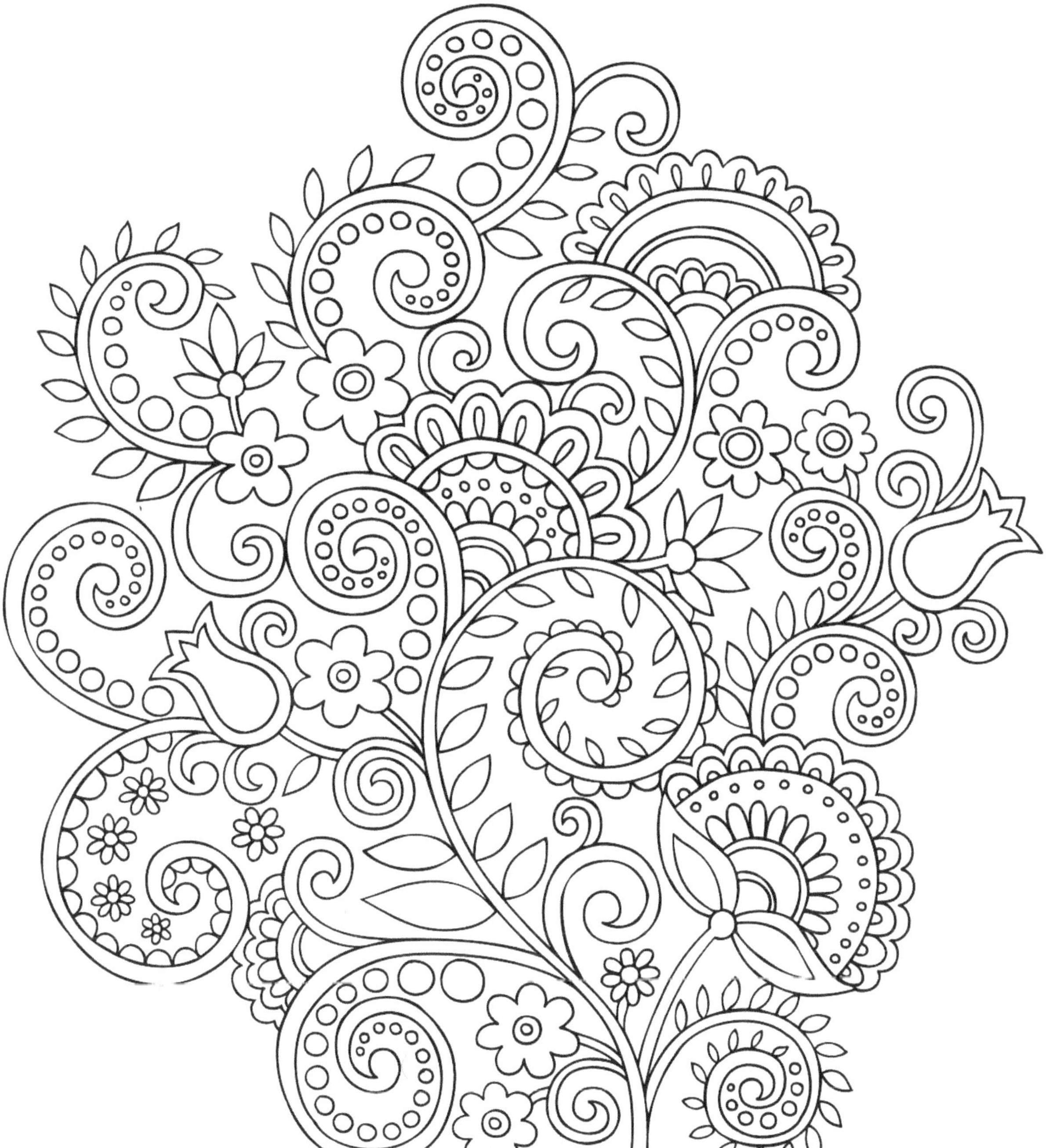

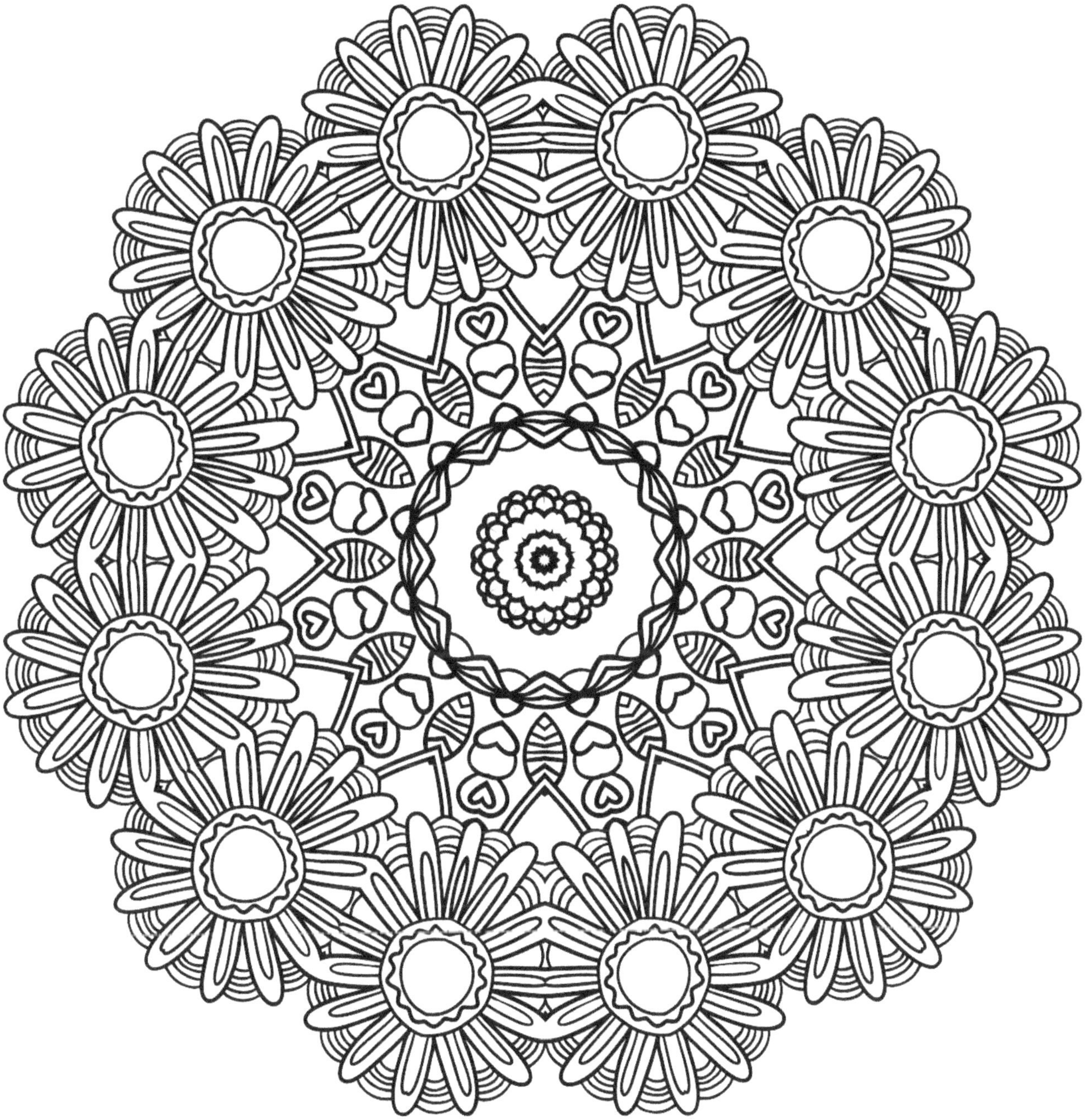

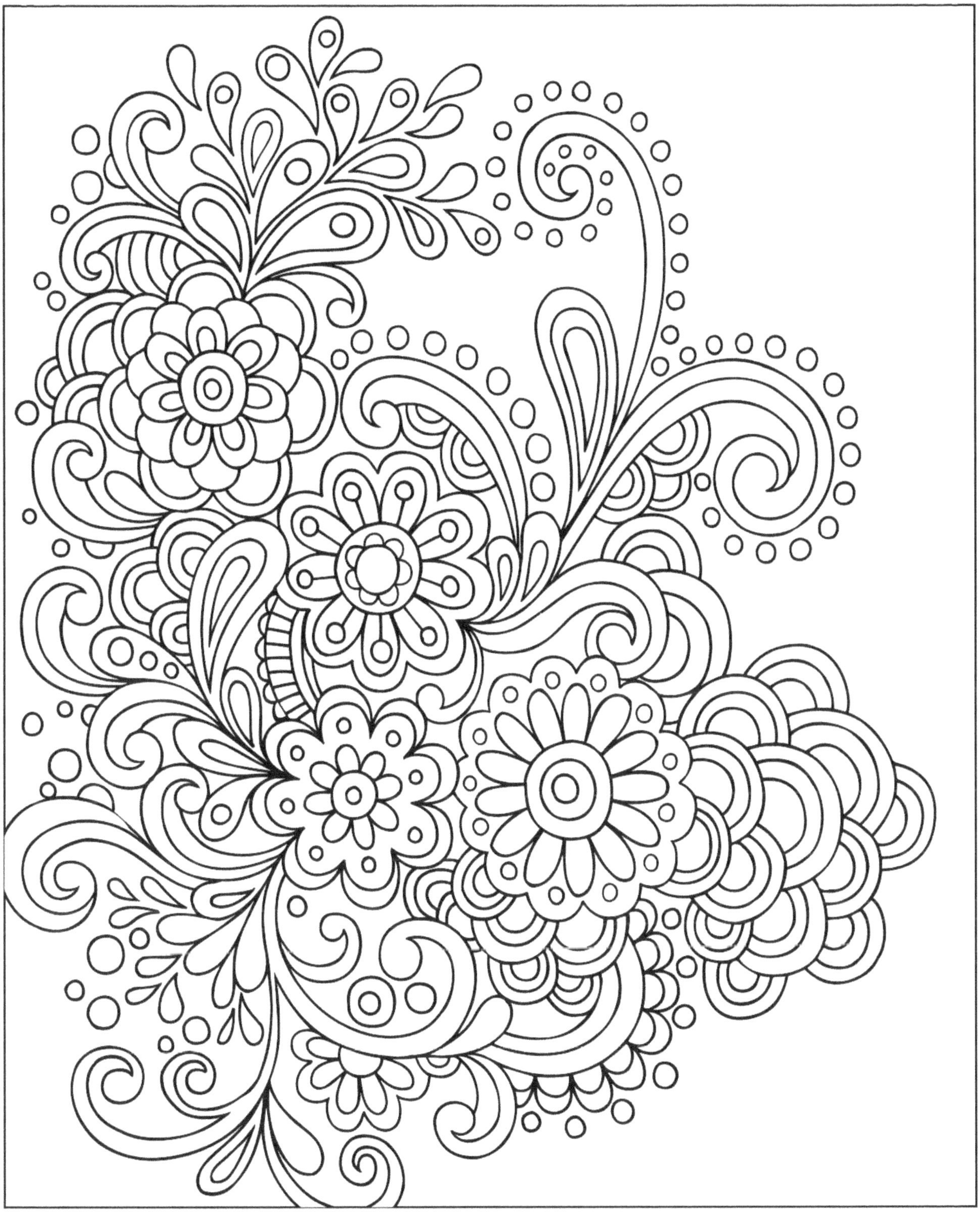

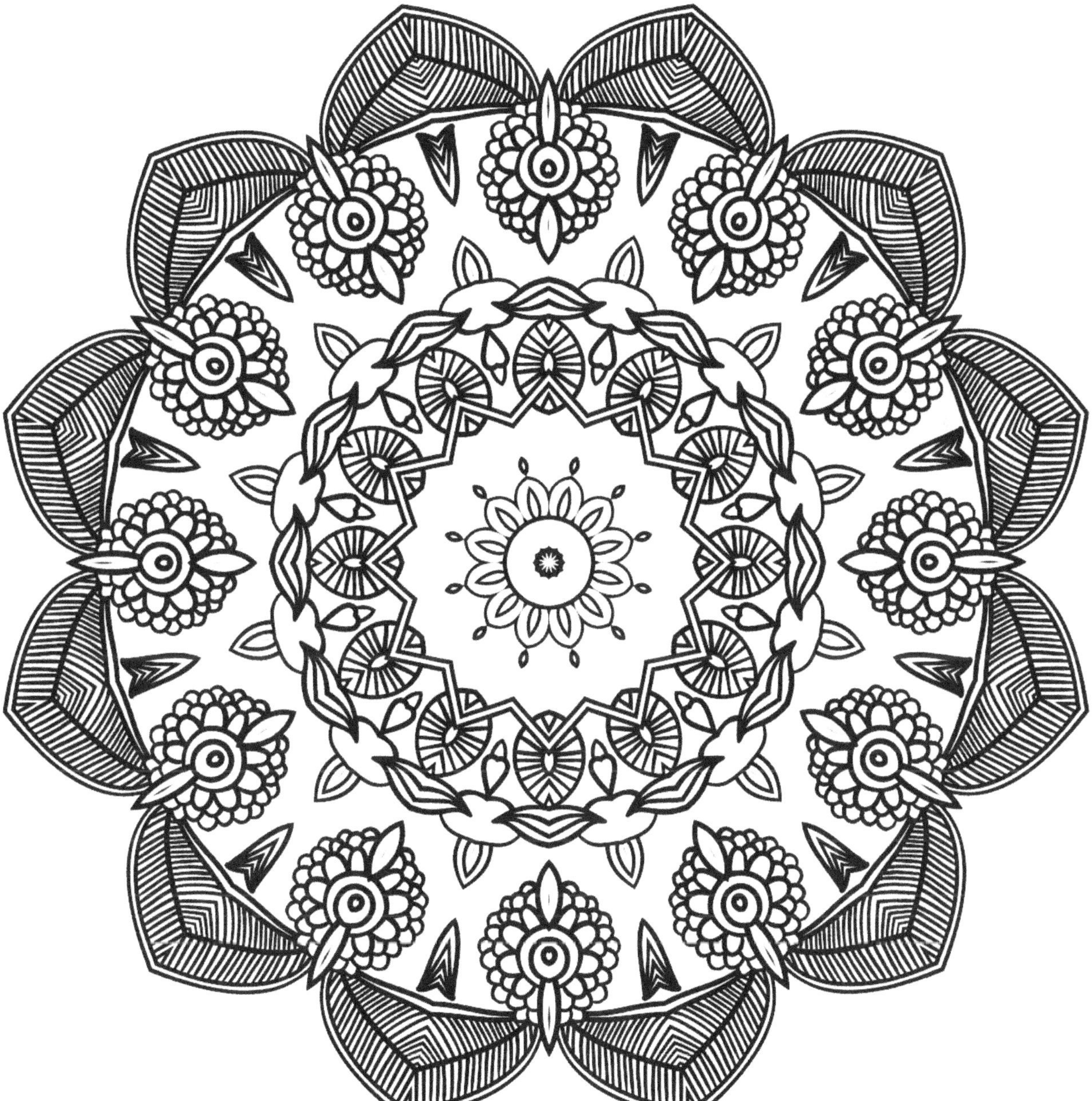

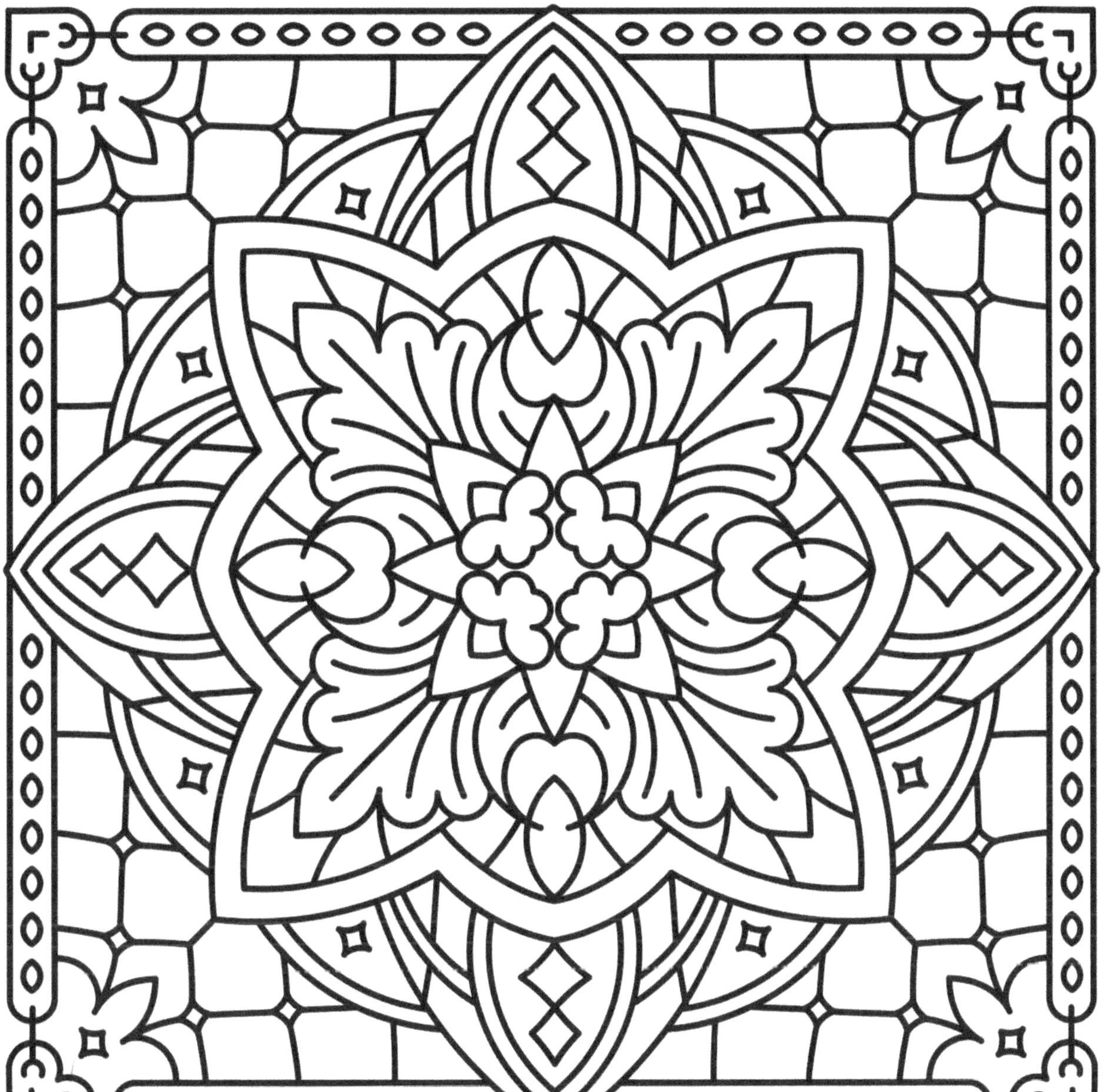

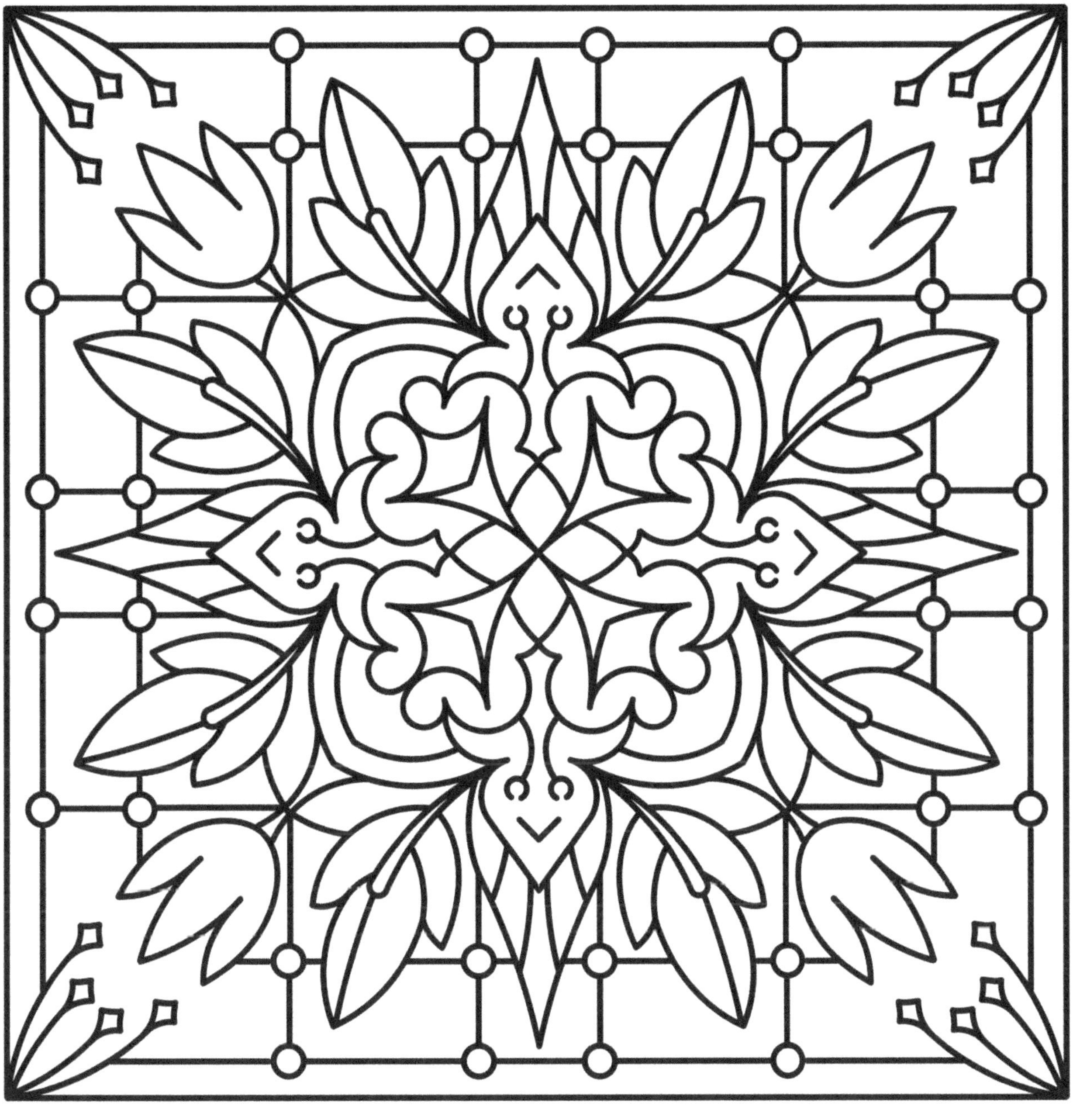

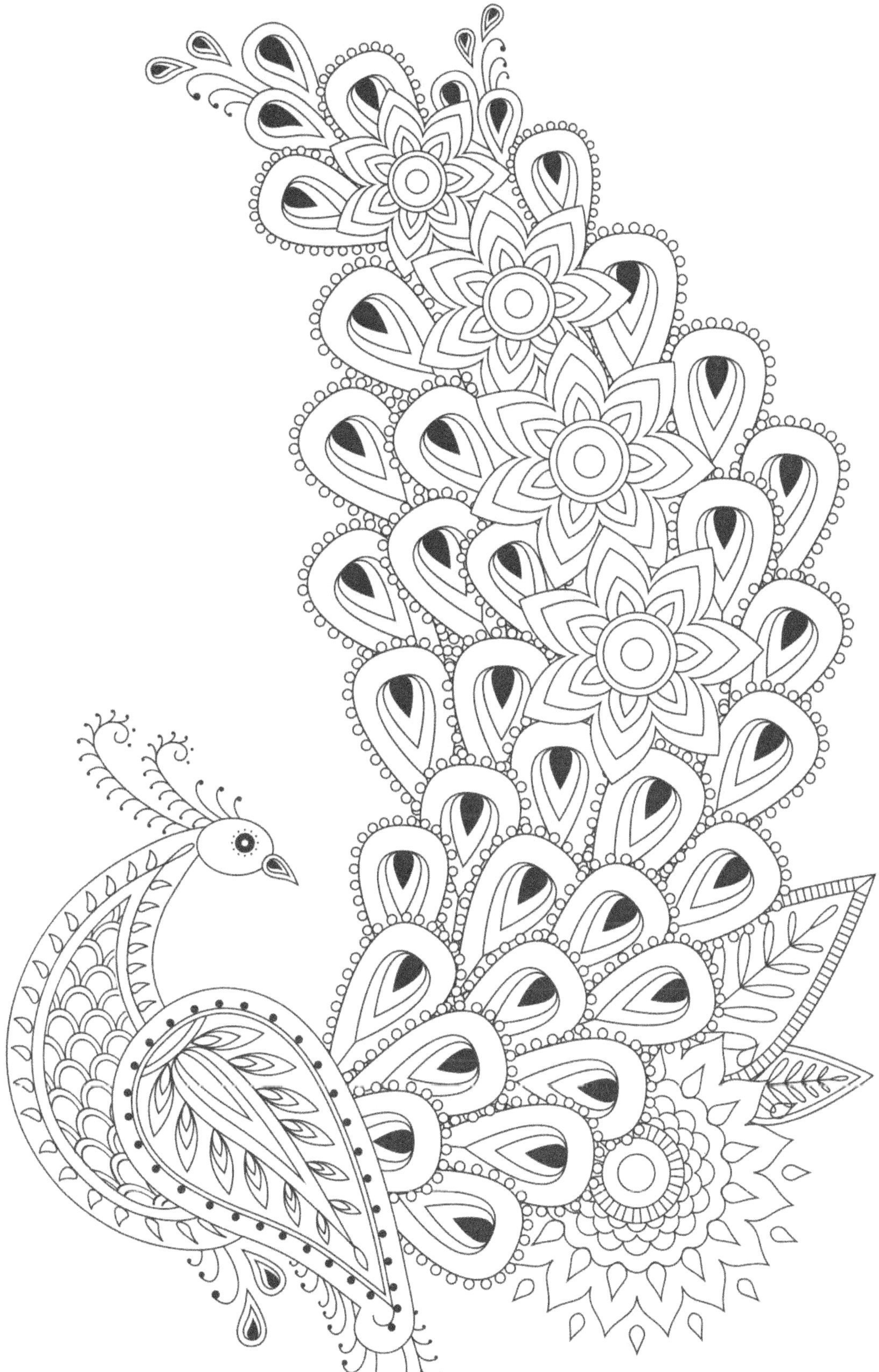

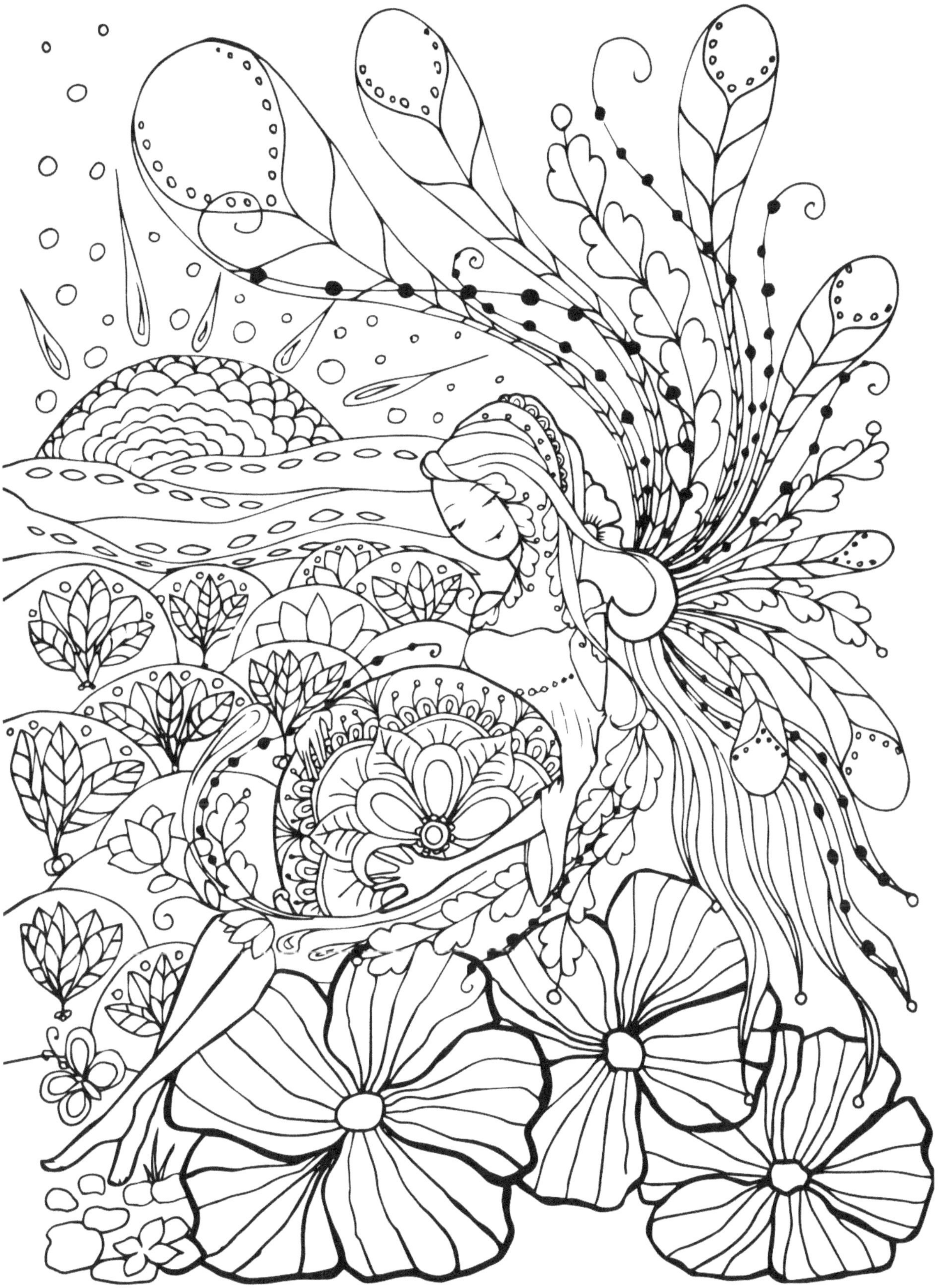

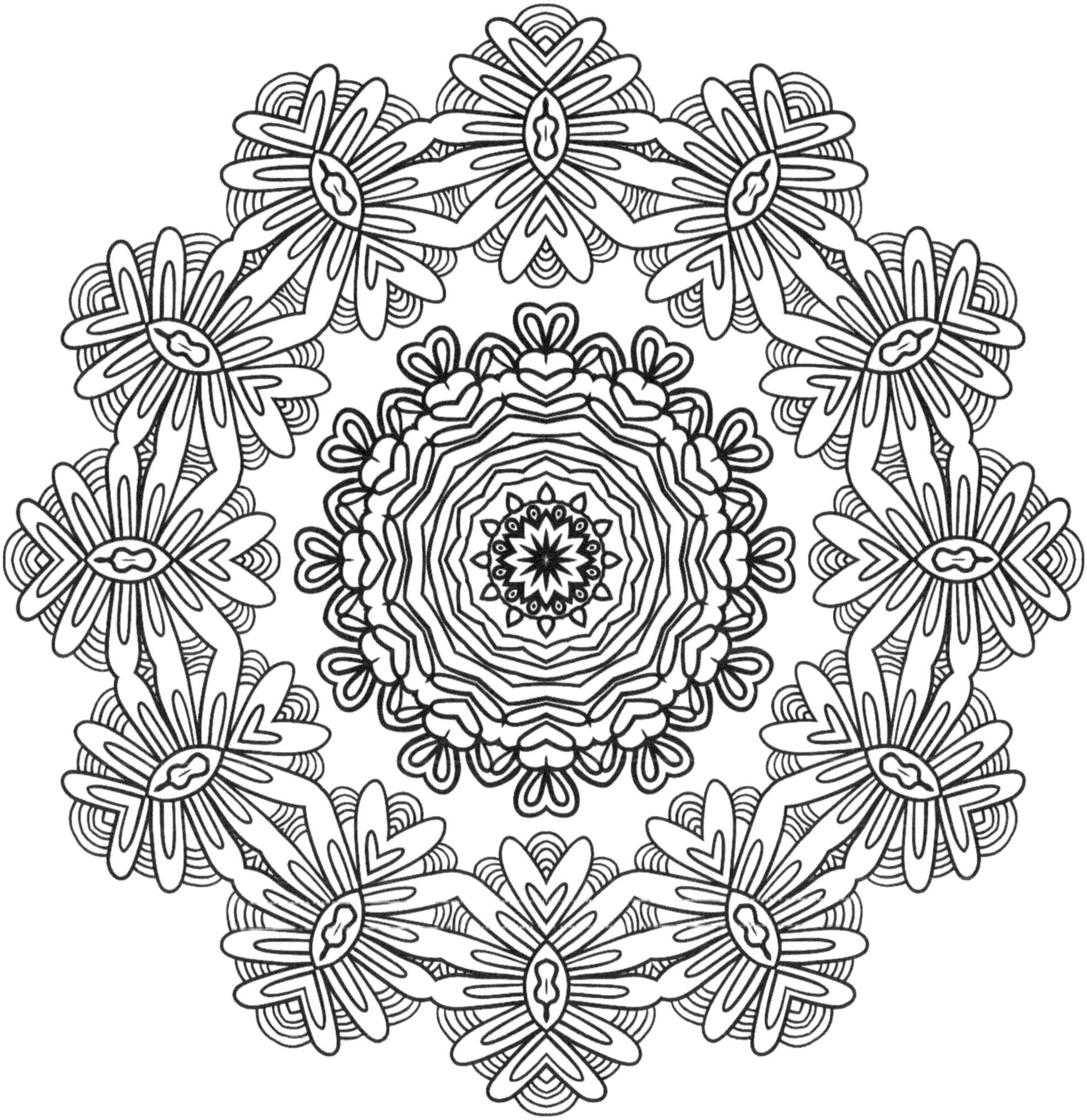

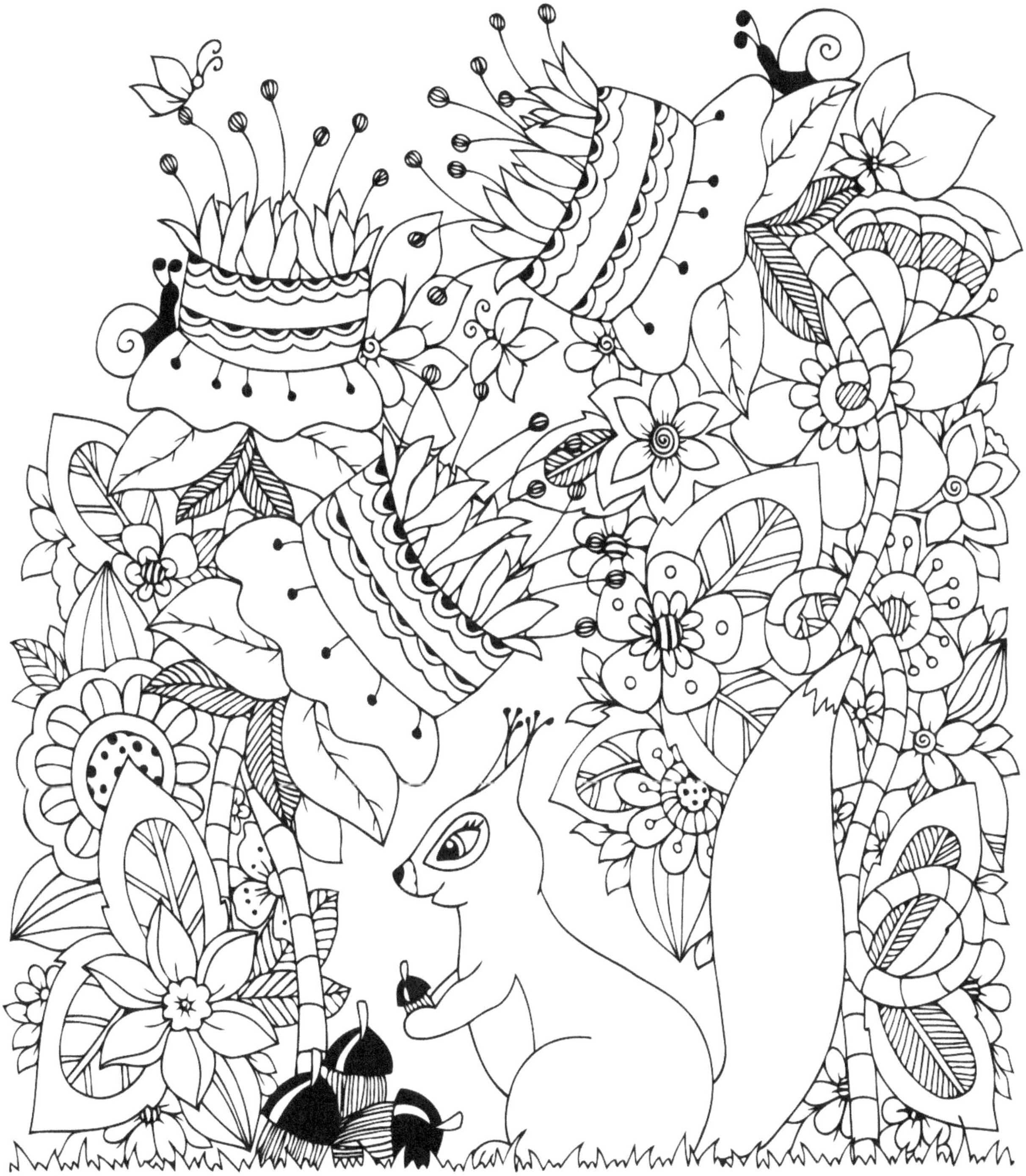

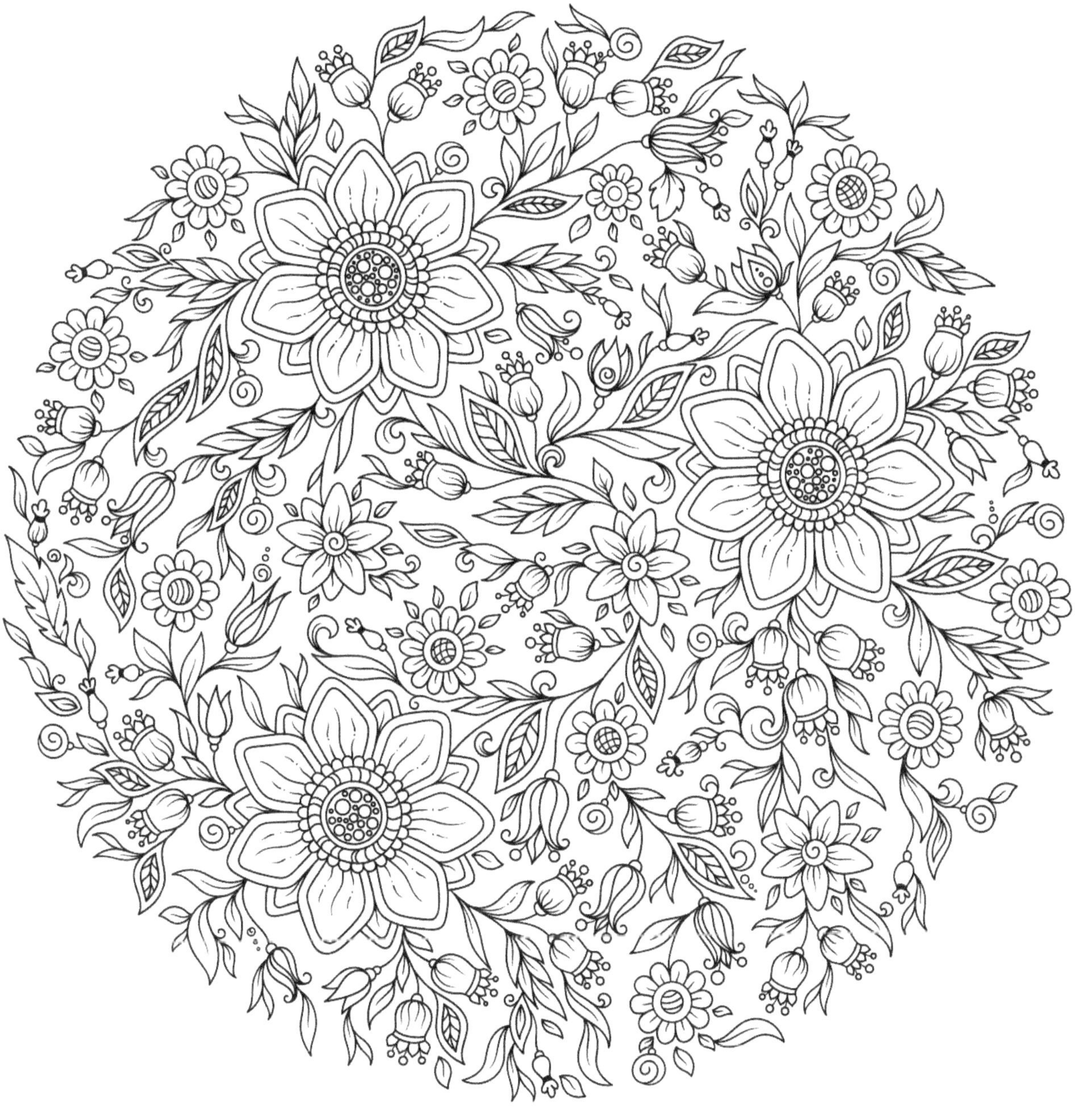

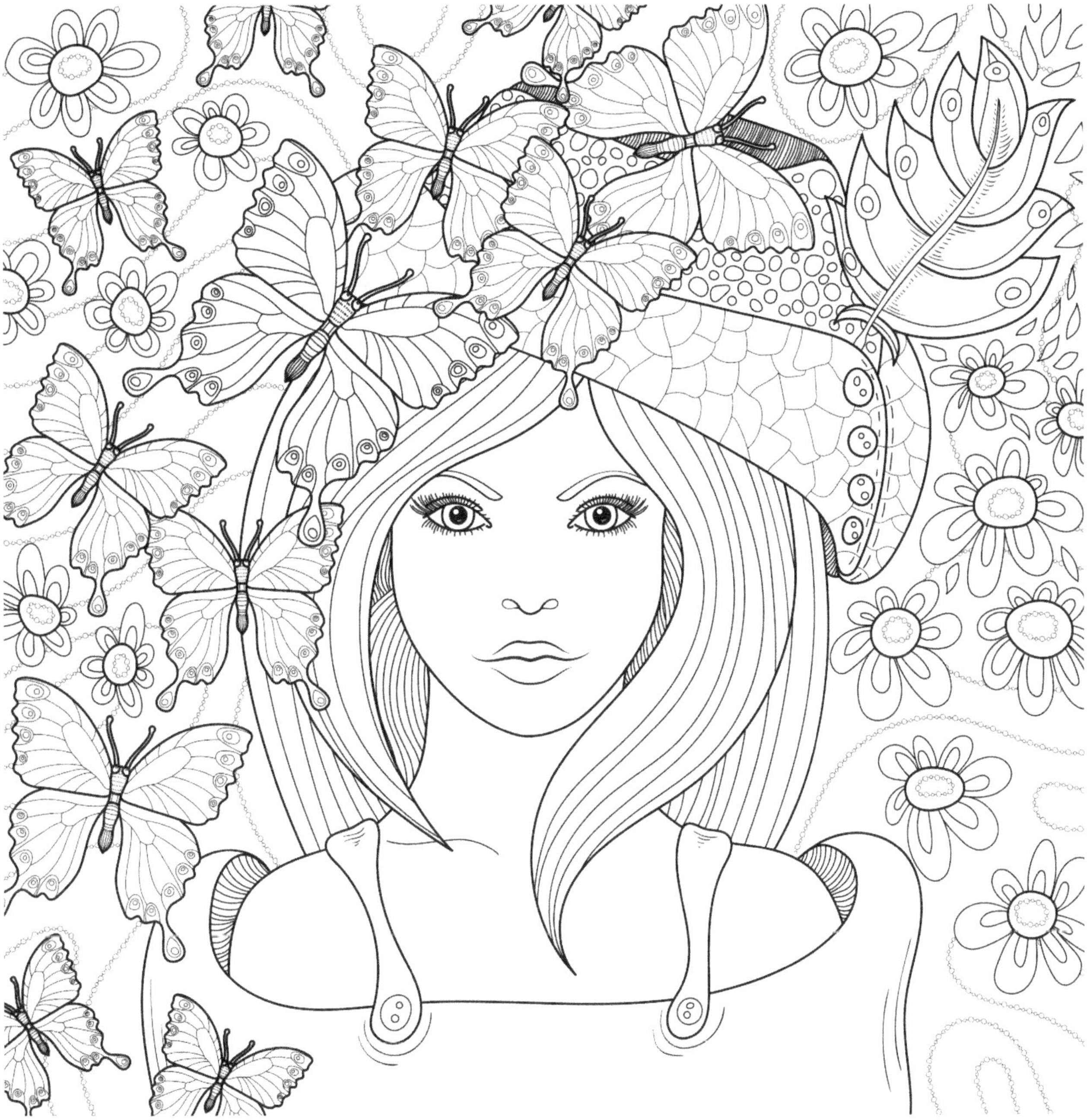

www.ingramcontent.com/pod-product-compliance
Lightning Source LLC
Chambersburg PA
CBHW081248180526
45170CB00007B/2345